STOP

MANAGING
AND
LEAD

Change Your Role, Change Your Results

DAVID RYE

D0064302

BUSINESS

AVON, MASSACHUSETTS

Published by Adams Business, an imprint of
Adams Media, a division of F+W Media, Inc.
57 Littlefield Street, Avon, MA 02322. U.S.A.
www.adamsmedia.com

ISBN 10: 1-59869-927-X
ISBN 13: 978-1-59869-927-2

Printed in the United States of America.

J I H G F E D C B A

Library of Congress Cataloging-in-Publication Data
is available from the publisher.

This publication is designed to provide accurate and authoritative information
with regard to the subject matter covered. It is sold with the understanding
that the publisher is not engaged in rendering legal, accounting, or other
professional advice. If legal advice or other expert assistance is required, the
services of a competent professional person should be sought.
—From a *Declaration of Principles* jointly adopted by a Committee of the
American Bar Association and a Committee of Publishers and Associations

Many of the designations used by manufacturers and sellers to distinguish
their product are claimed as trademarks. Where those designations appear
in this book and Adams Media was aware of a trademark claim, the designations have been printed with initial capital letters.

*This book is available at quantity discounts for bulk purchases.
For information, please call 1-800-289-0963.*

Contents

Introduction vii

Part I. Understanding Yourself | 1
1. Awakening the Leader in You 3
2. Do You Have What It Takes to Be a Leader? 19
3. Getting to Know Yourself. 29
4. Getting to Know the Four Personality Types 43
5. Developing an Empowered Personality 71

Part II. Leading Others | 83
6. Turning On with Goals. 85
7. Building Powerful Relationships 101
8. Motivating Your Organization. 119
9. Controlling Confrontations 139
10. Coaching Your Team 161

Part III. Your Career as a Leader | 183
11. Persuading Your Peers 185
12. Influencing Your Boss. 205
13. Inspiring Upper Management 231

Conclusion 250
Appendix: Glossary 251
Index 262

Acknowledgments

Without the help of my literary agent, Michael Snell, this book would never have been written. He worked with the publisher, prompted me, and, most important, motivated me to push for the assignment. Through all of the challenges associated with the project, he never lost his patience or sense of humor. Thank you to Peter Archer for working with me to get this project accepted by the publisher, Adams Media. For all your help, I am extremely grateful.

A special thanks goes to my wife, Marcia, who helped me with this project from its inception with her motivation and inspiration. She took care of the many details of the manuscript preparation and put up with my sometimes grouchy moods after numerous late nights of working on the final draft. I love her for everything she did.

Introduction

GREAT LEADERS HAVE always fascinated us by their innate ability to inspire the best in people. The fundamental purpose of *Stop Managing and Lead* is to show managers how to use the power that's built into your personality to lead others to get extraordinary things done. It's about the unique practices leaders use to transform visions into realities, and how they persuade, motivate, and inspire others to follow their lead to accomplish great things. This book will show you how leaders are able to turn everyday problems into exciting opportunities. Above all, it's about turning you from a manager into a leader.

From the outset, the book thrusts you into a series of challenging management situations where you're confronted by a wide variety of human behavior. You'll discover the attributes of your character and how to use the power that's inherent in your personality to become a truly effective leader, one that people will want to emulate and follow. Along the way, you'll learn how the different personality types of the people in your organization influence the way in which they interact with you and with one another. Once you know how to effectively interact with the different personality types, you will succeed beyond your wildest dreams at establishing important relationships and promoting yourself as a leader. As an added bonus, you will learn the secret of developing a motivational power within yourself that you never thought was possible.

We all have the mental wiring within us to become exemplary leaders. The qualities essential for effective leadership are wired into the personality of every human being, but in many this potential is dormant, waiting to be discovered. If you want to awaken your leadership qualities, go through the steps that are covered in the first three chapters of the book. You'll get to know who you really are and discover the leadership attributes inherent in you. During this process, you will learn how to use your personality as a master key to open countless opportunities for yourself.

Stop Managing and Lead provides the tools and step-by-step guidance you will need to evaluate your strengths, identify your blind spots, and plan a course of action for mastering your leadership competencies. When you dive into this book, you may find that you are able to breeze easily through several chapters at a time. You may even be able to knock out the whole book in one sitting because it's fun to read. Resist that temptation. Take your time. *Stop Managing and Lead* is designed to be absorbed strategically and methodically.

Live with the book for a while. Read a chapter; then give it some thought. Reflect on the various subjects discussed. If the theme of a chapter touches on one of your weaker areas, spend some time addressing the issues before you move on to the next chapter. Acquiring leadership is a step-by-step process. You have to develop it on the inside, before your leadership traits show on the outside. When that happens, people will follow you wherever you want to go.

Understanding Yourself

IT ALL STARTS with understanding yourself. Do you have the driving forces within your personality that will give you the courage and motivation to successfully become a leader? Part I addresses this issue. It forms the foundation for the rest of the book. Chapters 1 through 4 explain how to lay this foundation.

Everyone has the potential to become a leader. If you want to be one, wake up and move to the starting line. Along the way, you'll need to answer some tough questions to help you determine if you are ready to become a leader people will want to follow. What do you know about your personality? What are your leadership strengths and weaknesses? What do you know about the personality attributes of the people you'll be working with to reach your leadership goals? You'll learn how to know yourself, and from there to recognize the personality types of others so that you can influence their thinking and actions.

Indispensable Leadership Qualities

COMMITMENT	Leaders have a passion for committing to what they say they'll do with integrity both now and in the future.
COMMUNICATION	Leaders know how to speak from the heart and verbally communicate their thoughts so that they're understood by others.
COMPETENCE	Leaders know how to develop an active learning program that enhances their competency in everything they do.

CHAPTER 1

Awakening the Leader in You

Leadership is the capacity to inspire and rally people to endorse a common cause.

THE WORD "LEADERSHIP" wasn't a part of the English language until the early 1800s and at the time there was confusion about what it meant. It took 100 years before social scientists undertook serious studies of the phenomenon of leadership. It has only been over the past thirty years that researchers have made a lot of progress in determining how people become effective leaders—although this is still an ongoing area of study. We used to think that leaders were born and not made. Back in the old days, when strong social class barriers made it next to impossible for anyone to become a leader, we were trained to think that leadership was inherited. If your name wasn't Rockefeller, Firestone, Rothschild, or some other famous family name, you were not destined to become a leader.

As class barriers crumbled and leaders arose from all parts of society, it became clear that leadership required more than being born into the right family. We began to realize that everybody has the potential of becoming a leader, if they're given the chance. In this chapter, you will discover what leadership qualities you need to develop to catapult yourself into a leadership position.

INDISPENSABLE LEADERSHIP QUALITIES

Leaders display their leadership qualities through the way they think and display their commitment to life and through their ability to communicate from the heart with competence. To effectively show the behavior they expect from others and create a vision behind which to rally their followers, leaders must be clear about their own guiding principles first. They demonstrate their values through action and are prepared to stand up for their beliefs. In the process, leaders forge ahead to find support to achieve their goals and objectives.

In this chapter, we will look at how the process of leadership evolves using commitment, communication, and competence. When leaders do extraordinary things in their organization, they are always committed to their goals, communicating their vision with clarity, and displaying a level of competence that excites their constituents. Let's explore the attributes that make up each of these qualities.

COMMITMENT

We have all known people who want everything to be perfect in their eyes before they will commit to anything. As a result, they seldom make commitments. The uncommitted typically have no goals and quit when the going gets tough. A leader, on the other hand, understands that you can't achieve anything unless you are willing to make a commitment first. A leader readily commits to work hard to reach his goals. Bill Lear is such a leader.

If you've ever driven by a municipal airport, you have probably seen corporate jets taking off and landing. These small, very fast aircraft can carry only a handful of passengers. Many are Lear Jets, named after their inventor Bill Lear, who began developing his amazing jet in the 1950s. It took him several years to make his vision become a reality, but in 1964 his company delivered its first Lear Jet. Bill Lear's success as an aviation leader was immediate. His company sold every jet it was capable of producing.

However, not long after he started, Lear learned that two of his aircraft had crashed under mysterious circumstances. He immediately notified all of the Lear jet owners to ground their planes until his team could determine what had caused the crashes. When they discovered that a mechanical failure had caused the two jets to crash, they corrected the problem on all of the grounded jets. This cost Lear millions of dollars. It took the company several years to overcome the bad publicity it received from the incident. Bill Lear was willing to risk his success and fortune to correct an unfortunate incident. He demonstrated that he was committed to do what was best for his organization and his customers as well.

How a leader deals with unexpected events tells you a lot about who he really is. Although a crisis situation doesn't necessarily define a leader, it can certainly reveal many of his core qualities. Adversity creates crossroads that force a person to choose which path to take—the one that supports his convictions or the one that compromises those convictions. If he chooses to support his convictions as Bill Lear did, he becomes a stronger leader, even if that choice brings about negative consequences for the company.

Qualities of Commitment

As you continue on your journey up the leadership ladder, remember that each step in the ladder is placed there to hold your foot just long enough to allow you time to step up to the next higher rung. It wasn't put there as a footrest. There's an enormous amount of surplus reserve in each of us. But, that reserve is worthless unless you know how to use it. Persistence and effort are vitally important to your leadership campaign and your level of commitment to become a leader.

All leaders face plenty of obstacles and opponents. There will be times when reliance on your commitment will be the only thing that carries you forward. No matter how many times you get knocked down, commitment is what will get you back on your feet again. If you want to get anywhere worthwhile, you have got to be willing to get up and press on to whatever you're committed to do.

Commitment can be displayed in a wide range of activities: the goals you choose to work on, what you do to improve yourself, or the good things you choose to do for your associates. Commitment means different things to different people. To a marathoner, it means running another ten miles when her strength is gone. To a soldier, it's going over a hill, not knowing what's waiting on the other side. To a missionary, it's giving up his own comforts to make life better for others. To a leader, it's all of that and more because she is committed to leading people who depend on her.

Improving Your Ability to Commit

Boxer George Foreman once said, "Although we all get tired and discouraged when things are tough, you fight one more round if you want to be the champion or the leader of the pack. A second wind isn't good enough. You'd better have a third, a fourth, or as many winds as it takes to win. You only fail when you give up." He was committed, and he never gave up.

Leaders know how to set good examples in everything they do, and they live by what they practice. Exemplary leaders know that if they want to gain a commitment and achieve the highest standards from their followers, they display the same behavior. They're committed to being excellent role models.

In the final analysis, the only real measure of commitment is action. You commit to something, set up the steps to get it done, and make it happen. Leaders know the importance of following through on any commitments that they make because such actions inspire people to follow them. Here are several ways to improve your level of commitment:

Commit to commit. Every leader must ask, "What am I willing to commit to now and in the future?" If it came down to it, what in life would you not be able to stop doing, regardless of the consequences? Spend some time meditating on that and write down what you discover. Do your past actions match your ideals? Have you been reaching the goals you set for yourself? Are you achieving all that you believe you can? Do people believe in you, and are they willing to follow you? If your answer to any of these questions is no, ask yourself if the problem was your own lack of commitment.

Commit from the heart. Some people want to know what they'll achieve before they are willing to commit to something. They don't understand that commitment always precedes achievement. It starts when you look into your heart to see if you are really ready to commit to something that's important to you and the people you care about. When you can make a commitment from the heart and you're prepared to go all the way because you understand the depth of the commitment you've made, then you're well on your way to becoming a leader.

Commit to doing it. It's one thing to talk about making a commitment. It's another thing to actually do something about it. How are you at following through on your commitments? If you're having a problem taking the first step toward making a commitment, try doing what Thomas Edison did. When he had a good idea for an invention, he called a press conference to announce it. He made a public statement of his commitment to his invention. After the press conference was over, he went back into his lab and began work on the project. You don't have to call a press conference, but let your coworkers, employees, and supervisors know what your goals are. By making your commitments public, you will be more committed to following through on them.

Commit to win. When you make a commitment from your heart and take action steps, obstacles are bound to crop up. There will be times when your commitment is the only thing that carries you forward. Always remember that commitment is the enemy of failure. It is the promise that you have made to yourself to press on, to win the game no matter how tough the competition may be. Commitment is the backbone that makes great leaders winners. George Foreman once said, "If you keep getting up when you get knocked down, you will always be a winner."

Write it down. Create a written plan about what you are committed to do, both in the short and long term. Talk to some of the people who were the recipients of past commitments you've made (positive and negative) to solicit their advice. They may be able to offer you valuable ideas that you haven't thought of to improve upon your ability to commitment with conviction and delivery.

COMMUNICATIONS

Many American presidents have made a lasting impact on our country as great communicators who know how to deliver their message. Who can forget John F. Kennedy's immortal words: "Ask not what your country can do for you—ask what you can do for your country" or Teddy Roosevelt's classic statement: "Walk softly and carry a big stick"? Ronald Reagan's talent as an excellent communicator was revealed early in his career as a radio announcer. In his early twenties, he quickly became one of the best-known announcers in the Midwest. Throughout his career, Reagan displayed an uncommon ability to connect and communicate with people. When he announced his candidacy for president in 1980 and debated incumbent Jimmy Carter, he came across as a relaxed, likable, and competent leader. After the debate, a reporter asked if he had been nervous debating the president. Reagan answered, "No, not at all. Heck, I've been on the same stage with John Wayne."

Reagan would go down in history as a good president because he possessed a clear vision, made decisions easily, and delegated his authority very effectively. But, he was a great leader because of his uncanny ability to communicate to people in all walks of life. People always knew who he was, what he stood for, and what he wanted to do. His strength as a communicator made him the kind of leader that people wanted to follow.

Developing excellent communication skills is essential to becoming an effective leader. You must be able to communicate your ideas in a style that will produce both enthusiasm and inspiration in others. Having the most important message in the world doesn't matter if no one can understand it. A leader's eloquent speech about her vision, however, isn't nearly enough. Her deeds are far more important than her words. When someone wants to determine how committed a leader really is, he wants to know what she's done and not what she says she's going to do. A leader's words and deeds must be consistent with the commitments she makes.

Qualities of Communication

Even if you don't plan to become president of the United States, you still need to possess the ability to communicate. The success of your personal and professional life depends on it. People will not follow you if they don't know what you're saying or want to do. Good leaders encourage people to tell them what they need to know first, so they have the benefit of that knowledge before they speak. Leaders know how to interact with their followers and are willing to take the time to get to know each one by listening to what he or she has to say.

An unwillingness to listen is a common problem among poor leaders, which was demonstrated by George W. Bush. According to Jacob Weisberg's book, *The Bush Tragedy*, the president's administrative staff was instructed to tell him only what he wanted to hear; otherwise he wouldn't listen.

When was the last time you really paid close attention to what someone was saying to you? Do more than grab onto just the theme or facts that he is telling you. Listen not only to his words, but also watch his body language so you get his complete message. Repeat what you believe you heard and ask him to verify your understanding of what he said. Include a positive affirmation after he is finished speaking. For example, if a person is nervously twitching his body and speaking in a shaky voice when he addresses you, he is probably unsure of himself. If it's appropriate, provide him with a positive affirmation to help build his self-esteem.

Improving Your Communication Skills

Leadership is a dialogue, not a monologue. To enlist support, leaders must have an intimate knowledge of people's dreams and be able to breathe life into the hopes of their constituents. Leaders do this by forging a unity of purpose that shows that their dreams will benefit the entire organization. They're experts at inspiring others with their enthusiasm to achieve the vision and dreams of individuals and groups as well. They communicate their passion in an expressive style and clear, vivid language.

Developing excellent communication skills is essential to effective leadership. Without it, you will never become a leader. For example, you should regularly recognize the contributions made by your team members. You can communicate this recognition in a one-on-one setting or in a group setting. You can communicate it with dramatic gestures or by a simple statement. Leaders know how to show appreciation for their team members' contributions by celebrating their achievements in the most appropriate way.

You must be able to share your message with others in a manner that is clear to them and sparks their interest. Here are several pointers that will help you improve your communication skills:

Keep it simple. Communication is not just about what your words say but how you say it. Adding "fancy" words to make your message sound "important" will be ineffective if nobody understands what you're trying to say. If you really want to impress people, communicate with simplicity. Create an exciting opening statement that will grab the attention of your audience like, "Here is a sure-fire way to get your career moving on the fast track." Then, summarize what needs to be done to make it happen, and add a closing statement that will make people want to act. These "keep it simple" steps work just as well in one-on-one encounters as they do in group encounters.

Say it with meaning and purpose. Once you have assembled the words you want to say in your head, you must give voice to those words with meaning. You must be able to pitch your voice and your tone so that everyone not only knows what you're saying but feels your excitement and commitment. Always remember that leadership is an art. Just like any other art form—whether it's painting, acting, or writing—leadership is a means of personal expression. To become a credible leader, you have to learn to express yourself in ways that are your own. You cannot lead through someone else's values or someone else's words.

Never lie. Liars can never be great communicators, even when they try to tell the truth, because nobody will believe whatever they say. To communicate effectively you must believe in what you are about to say. If you don't, no one else will. Ordinary people become extraordinary communicators when they are fired up with conviction and a belief in what they're saying. If you are forced to communicate a message to others that you don't believe is right, it will sound convoluted and insincere. When announcing a decision you don't agree with or have reservations about, you might say something like, "I have been asked to announce something that is outside of my control. The message from corporate headquarters is . . ." Your followers will know that their leader is just the messenger.

Seek responses. Always remember that the goal of communication is to solicit an action by the person or persons you're talking to. If you decide to dump a bunch of information on people, make sure they have what they'll need in order to respond to you with questions or answers. When you speak to people, give them a vision and the goals to achieve it.

Rate yourself. How do you rate your ability to communicate with others? When you talk to people, do you inspire and motivate them? If you can't tell, you are probably not communicating effectively. Are you able to consistently express a message that people understand? If action is required on their part, are they willing to do it? Are you able to connect to people in one-on-one encounters? How about group encounters? If you know in your heart that your message is great, yet people have a difficult time buying into it, you may have a problem communicating effectively. You may need to adjust your delivery style for your target audience.

Write clear messages. Take a moment and examine memos that you have recently written. Did you write short, to-the-point sentences, or did you meander? Were your readers able to grasp the importance of what you were trying to say in the first paragraph of your message? Did you use the fewest words possible to get your point across? When using written words, a communicator's best friend is simplicity and clarity.

Focus on your audience. In the past, has your communication focus been on you, your material, or your audience? If it has not been on your audience, you need to change your focus. Before you communicate with anyone (individual or group encounters), think about what his needs and desires are and what questions he might ask. For example, if your employees need to know where the company is going in the future and want to know how it all will affect them, then focus on these two issues up front when you address them.

Support what you say. Are there any discrepancies between what you say and what you do? Seek the counsel of a few trustworthy friends and ask them if they believe you are supporting what you say. They may see things that you are not aware of. Graciously accept any criticism they offer you, and adjust your communication techniques accordingly.

COMPETENCE

We all admire people who display high levels of competence. One such person was Thomas Jefferson. He was born April 13, 1743, in the foothills of the Blue Ridge Mountains in what was then regarded as a western province of the Old Dominion. By all accounts he was an obsessive student, often spending fifteen hours a day with his books. Jefferson always thought of himself as an ordinary citizen. He worked hard, lived a simple life, and at age twenty, started his own drafting business.

Had Jefferson been content to work his drafting trade, he probably would not have made it into the history books. He chose to live an extraordinary life as a leader of the movement for American independence and coauthor of the Declaration of Independence with John Adams and Benjamin Franklin. Jefferson's competence allowed him to excel at everything he touched and wrote. You too can excel and become a leader in whatever area you choose, as long as you are competent in whatever you do.

Harry S. Truman was another man who never gave up in his drive to find and develop his strongest area of competence. He was initially involved in an oil venture that ran out of money and oil. He left the oil business and started a clothing store, which didn't do any better than his oil venture. As a result, he went broke, but he wasn't discouraged. Later in his life, he got involved in politics. Historians are already saying nice things about Truman, the multiple-time failure who finally found his competence as president of the United States. He was committed, in spite of his failures, because he learned from his mistakes, and he became one of the most competent presidents in history.

Qualities of Competence

Competence to a leader is his ability to plan something and then do it in such a way that others have confidence in what he's doing. Grand dreams don't become realities through the actions of a leader unless they're backed by his constituents' confidence in his competence. Because of their competence, leaders can inspire people and rally them to support a cause. All highly competent leaders continually search for ways to become better at everything they do. It's a vital part of their self-improvement process. As they go through their self-directed learning cycle, they inspire and motivate others to do the same thing. Effective leaders rely on their drive for learning to supplement and increase their overall level of competence. They are comfortable with the fact that they are accountable for the consequences of their decisions and actions. They're constantly improving on what they know works and correcting what doesn't work. Good is never enough for them; they spur themselves to rise to the next level.

Improving Your Level of Competence

Highly competent people are dependable and always show up for a job when they're expected to. However, they don't show up in body alone. They come ready to work, no matter how they feel, what circumstances they're about to face, or how difficult they expect a situation to be. They can be counted on to always go the extra mile to fulfill commitments that they have made to the people they support.

Where do you stand when it comes to getting the job done? Do you attack everything you do with fervor and perform it at the highest competence level possible? Or is okay sometimes good enough for you? Are you one of those competent people who can see what needs to be done before anyone else does? Are you the one who makes it happen? Are you a thinker, a doer, or a let's-see-what-happens player? The more competent you are the greater influence you will have on your organization. Here are several ways to improve upon your level of competence:

Get involved. If you have been mentally or emotionally detached from your work, it is time to reconnect. Giving what you're doing at work an appropriate amount of your undivided attention. Sit back for a moment and figure out why you've been detached. Do you need new challenges? Are you having recurring conflicts with your boss or coworkers? Are you in a dead-end job? Identify the sources of your problems, and create a plan to resolve them.

Raise your standards. If you believe you're not performing at a consistently high standard of competence, re-examine your current standards. Are you shooting too low (i.e., just good enough)? Do you consistently cut corners? If this is the case, hit the mental reset button in your brain and start demanding better things from yourself.

Practice self improvement. Identify three to five things you can do to improve your professional skills. Set up what you've identified as goals, and dedicate whatever it takes to follow through on them.

Search for flaws. Look at the major events of your life including those involving family, friends, and work-related relationships, and examine where you might have cut corners, compromised your beliefs, or let people down. Recall every instance that you can over the past several months. Then, sit back and reflect on what you could have done to effect different outcomes. What can you do in the future to avoid your past competence flaws? Does the same problem keep surfacing? Detectable patterns will help you diagnose competence issues. That's the easy part. Now, make plans and set goals to do something about it.

Create a vision. A vision is a compelling image of an achievable future event or outcome. It may be grand in scope, but it must be achievable. Nobody can become a competent leader without a personal vision. You can't give direction to your organization if your people don't share your vision. It has to be bigger than you if you want them to help you achieve your vision and it has to be for the greater good of your organization. It's what they see in your vision for the organization and themselves that fuels their drive to support your vision.

PUTTING IT ALL TOGETHER

In this chapter, I introduced you to three indispensable qualities of a leader—commitment, communication, and competence. I gave you guidelines to further your development of these qualities in yourself. Each of us has a different interpersonal style when it comes to applying any of the indispensable leadership qualities.

Based on your interpersonal style, how can you best apply the attributes of your personality to enhance your leadership skills? How do you react to different situations, conscious choices, and communicate with others in your domain? To answer these and other important personality-related questions, it would help if you knew what type of personality you have. In the next two chapters I'll help you determine your personality type. You will have an opportunity to answer some tough questions and take a personality quiz that will help you get to know yourself in a different light. You'll discover how to apply the attributes of your personality to significantly improve your leadership qualities.

CHAPTER 2

Do You Have What It Takes to Be a Leader?

The first and most important person you must learn to lead is yourself.

LET'S FACE IT: If you're honest with yourself, you have always wanted to lead the parade rather than being stuck between two tuba players, playing a flute that nobody can hear. If you're ready to become a leader, where do you start? You start by learning to lead yourself.

Let's start with the incredible Wal-Mart story. Although he has been called many things, including an enemy of small-town America, Sam Walton is widely recognized as one of the greatest business leaders of all times.

He opened his first Wal-Mart store in the small town of Rogers, Arkansas, in 1962. "At the time, we really only had two choices," Walton recalls. "We could stay in our small-town store and be devoured by the discounting wave that was sweeping the country, or we could open a discount store in our small town. I choose to do the latter." When he died in 1992, there were 1,700 Wal-Mart stores throughout the country.

While other retailers were complaining about the competition, Walton was solving the problem with innovation. He was willing to start a discount store, even though there was no precedent for it and no one knew how Arkansas (or the rest of the country) would react to it.

No matter what industry leaders are in, they will face inevitable problems. Good leaders anticipate them and always leave behind a legacy of successors who follow the leader's initial vision. After his death, Sam Walton's leadership team built Wal-Mart into the largest corporation in the world. They, too, had what it takes to be leaders, thanks to Sam Walton's vision and training.

DO YOU HAVE WHAT IT TAKES?

Becoming a leader has always been a process. The tools leaders use are unlike those of other occupations. Engineers have computers, artists have paint and brushes, musicians have instruments, and so on. Leaders have no tools—at least no tangible ones. The art of leadership comes from mastering one's self through self-development. It's not about stuffing a whole bunch of new information into your head or trying out the latest management fad. It's about leading from your heart, about liberating the leadership attributes that are built into your personality. It's about setting yourself on fire to accomplish great things.

Leading is about doing what you care about. Your quest must begin with an inner journey to discover who you are and what you really want to do with your life. As you go through the self-development steps in this book, you will develop your confidence to lead. Self-confidence is really an awareness of who you are and the faith you have in the power of your personality to achieve great things. Along the way, you must wrestle with some difficult questions:

How certain am I of my own conviction to become a leader?

The keys to your success are your priorities and the level of your concentration. People who want to become leaders know what their priorities are and concentrate on getting them done. If you have concentration but no priorities, you won't accomplish anything. Harness the two together and leadership will be in your grasp. Focus on your strengths. Cultivate your relationships with others who can help you develop your leadership skills.

How prepared am I to handle complex problems?

To get a jump on your leadership goals, turn yourself into a problem solver. Problems are where the real opportunities can be found in any organization, and they're everywhere if you know where to look for them. For every problem your organization has, there is an opportunity for somebody who can come up with a solution. Companies recognize employees who provide solutions.

Since you can't offer a solution until you know about a problem, how do you find them in your organization?

Listen and activate your peripheral vision wherever you go. When you hear an executive say, "Boy, do we need to fix that," step in and ask, "What do we need to fix?" Ask your boss questions: "If there was one problem that you would like to see resolved, what would it be? What are some of the biggest challenges our company faces?" The question is a powerful communication search tool for seeking out problems and opportunities.

Do I have enough confidence in myself to become a leader?

To become a leader you have to be confident that you can move mountains. If you lack the confidence to do that, step aside and watch someone else do it in your place. You can't motivate anyone to follow you if you don't believe you are worthy of being a leader. As a leader with confidence, you must stand on center stage and show your audience how to do things.

Does my organization want leaders?

You can't become a leader in an organization that doesn't want one. When you make an investment of your time and energy to become a leader, you must have confidence in your organization. Your time is one of your most valuable commodities. If you become involved in a leadership venture, it must be worth your total commitment. If you feel your organization doesn't want leaders, you are going to be hard-pressed to give it all the support it needs. If you don't have any confidence in your organization, join one that welcomes leadership candidates.

Am I a decision-maker?

You have to be a decision-maker if you want to be a leader. A leader is willing to assume the ultimate responsibility for her actions. The buck not only stops at her desk, it also starts from there. As a leader, you will often be on your own, and no one can make the tough decisions for you. You have to be a creative thinker who thrives in competitive situations and who knows how make tough decisions in a timely manner with confidence.

Do I know how to recognize opportunities?

Know how to recognize and take advantage of opportunities because nobody else will do it for you. Do you ever find yourself saying, "I should have done that. Why didn't I speak up?" You can't afford to allow opportunities to slip by you. Evaluate every opportunity that comes your way and ask yourself, "Is this an opportunity that will work for me and benefit my organization?"

Am I good at setting and meeting goals?

Goals are the fuel that gives you the energy to reach your objective. If you don't have precise, clearly defined goals, you will never make it as a leader. You'll be like a ship without a rudder drifting in the sea. When you set goals, something inside you should say, "Let's get going. What am I waiting for?" By setting goals you're laying the bricks in the foundation of your career. Since it's your future, why not think big? Leaders always think big when they set their goals. Goals need to be big enough to create excitement. That's one of the main purposes of a goal.

Can I keep a cool head when I'm under pressure?

If you get uptight, frustrated, and sometimes angry when you're under pressure, that's a problem. We all get upset when we're beset by pressure; that's only human. But if other people determine that you are so upset you're unable to control the situation, you are in trouble. A business leader must act in much the same way a military officer does when confronted with a crisis. If your troops are about to enter a battle, your mere presence must convey the message: "Our strategy is sound, and I am confident that we are ready to face this situation." Your followers will then be able to approach the problem with a winning attitude because you kept a cool head and demonstrated leadership under pressure.

Can I handle confrontations?

Confrontations result when a disagreement, a controversy, or a personal clash occurs between two or more people. The word itself connotes something serious, and for this reason, leaders avoid them as much as possible. As everybody knows from experience, confrontations are unpleasant, disruptive to relationships, and often counterproductive to organizations. Nobody walks away from an unresolved confrontation as a winner. Leaders know how to bring the conflict to the surface, how to acknowledge the feelings and views of all sides, then redirect the energy of everybody involved toward a shared solution. Often, a few minutes of listening can do wonders to defuse a confrontation. Even if you disagree with one of the parties, allow them to get their feelings out into the open so that you can address and hopefully dispel the reasons that caused the confrontation.

Do I have the emotional state of mind to become a leader?

People pay close attention to a leader's subtle expressions of emotion through body language and facial expression. Some emotions such as enthusiasm can quickly become contagious. Others, such as depression or discouragement, can drag down the entire organization. Leaders with positive emotional states of mind are like human magnets. People naturally gravitate to them and want to follow them. Such leaders inspire enthusiasm in their organizations and attract the best people to work for them. Conversely, leaders who emit negative emotional states of mind, who are irritable and domineering, repel people, and have few followers.

Do I have a leadership personality?

The type of personality you have plays a role in your development as a leader. For example, leaders typically have outgoing personalities, and many like to participate in outdoor sports and social functions. They're also creative individuals. You'll often find them involved in personal projects like remodeling their home or restoring a vintage sports car. They know how to channel their energy into work-related projects that motivate them and they'll get challenging jobs done in record time. If they are suddenly cast into an urgent turnaround situation, they can develop a commanding personality style that can be very effective at getting things done.

Am I committed to do whatever I set out to accomplish?

Many people make life unnecessarily difficult for themselves by dissipating their energy. Rather than make a commitment to do something, they waste their energy worrying about what they should be doing. As a result, they end up doing nothing. The word "worrying" means to be agitated or irritated. "Committing" is a take-charge word that neutralizes worrying. It's also the first step in the motivational process. You have to commit to something before you can motivate yourself to do it.

Am I willing to lead by example?

You can't ask your followers to walk on water for you if you choose to ride a luxury liner over the same route. If you want your team to put in fourteen-hour workdays when they're needed, make sure you're there with them. Leaders never ask their followers to do something they are not willing to do. If you're a manager, never ask an employee to act as your gofer. Let your employees know that they are all teammates playing on the same winning team with you and, as their manager, you will reward them if they do their best to meet company goals.

Do I really want to be a leader?

Do you want to share your inspired vision with others, enable others to participate with you, and follow your lead? If you are, then you want to be a leader. How much effort you are willing to expend to become a leader is directly related to how motivated you are, how committed to developing basic leadership skills.

Your answers to these questions and to those that arise from them will help augment your quest for leadership. The more you know about what leadership requires, the easier it will be for you to take on challenging opportunities with confidence. Actively seek to learn as much as you can about the political, economic, and social issues affecting your company. Ask lots of questions, and take the initiative to find the answers you need.

THE LEADERSHIP DEVELOPMENT PROCESS

Becoming a leader is a lot like investing in the stock market. If you think you're going to make a fortune in a day by investing in that hot stock your golf buddy told you about, you're not going to make it. The same goes for becoming a leader. Leadership develops over time, not in a day. It's what you do day after day over the long haul that will make you a leader. If you continually invest in your leadership skills and let your personal assets compound at a high rate of return, the inevitable result will be your growth into an outstanding leader.

At some early point in the process, you will discover that you don't know everything about leadership. You may look back and realize that no one is following you. Benjamin Franklin wisely commented, "To be conscious of the fact that you don't know as much as you thought you knew is a great step forward in your knowledge."

When you recognize your lack of leadership skills and make the effort to implement a daily development program, exciting things will begin to happen. Your call to lead can come at any time and in ways that you'd least expect. People will suddenly appear out of nowhere and ask for your opinions on a variety of subjects. You will start getting offers to head up group discussions or be a guest speaker at a prestigious event. In the process, you will start to develop the feeling that people trust you and respect your judgment.

Your success as a leader will be directly dependent on how well you get along with people and your ability to develop relationships that enable people to help you get extraordinary things done. When you dig deeper into the dynamics of leadership, you will uncover practices that are common in great leaders. Learn how to foster collaboration and build trust in your followers. Your sense of teamwork must reach beyond your direct reports or close confidants. Engage anyone who can help make the projects you're working on succeed. Once you're in the development phase, enlist others to participate in making it happen. Know how to motivate and inspire your constituents, have an intimate knowledge of their dreams, aspirations, values, and learn how to speak to them in their language.

Don't be afraid to experiment with new ideas and be willing to take risks. Despite the inevitability of mistakes and failures that are typically associated with innovation, accept new challenges, and proceed forward. Always be willing to step into the unknown to search for opportunities to innovate, grow, and improve. It's one of the best ways to learn how to become a great leader.

PUTTING IT ALL TOGETHER

Leaders often like to gaze across the horizon of time, imagining the attractive opportunities to pursue in the future. They like to make things happen, to change the way things are, and to create something no one else has ever done before. In some ways, leaders live their lives in a "play-forward" rather than a "play-back" mode. Before they start a project they see in their mind's eye what the result will look like, much like an architect makes a model of a skyscraper before he builds it. Their clear image of the future pulls them forward to create what they see in their vision.

Everyone has the potential to become a leader, but it isn't accomplished overnight. No matter where you're starting from, you will get better at leading over time. There are many complex facets of leadership, including experience, emotional strength, people skills, discipline, vision, and motivation. The many factors that come into play in leadership are what makes becoming a leader both challenging and rewarding.

CHAPTER 3

Getting to Know Yourself

One of man's greatest achievements was when he figured out a way to understand himself.

WE ALL TALK to a variety of people every day about lots of different personal and work-related subjects. Have you noticed how well you get along with some people? You find yourselves easily laughing at the same things, or discover that you have similar interests, likes, and dislikes. When you present these people with a problem, you both instantly zero in on the same solution.

Then there are those other people. It's a challenge to hold a conversation with them for more than a minute. For some reason, you're uncomfortable in their presence, guarding what you say. You can even become inexplicably hostile to them. You can't figure out why they don't get the importance of what you're trying to tell them. How do you persuade them to your way of thinking? How do you motivate them? Perhaps if you knew more about their personality, had a better understanding of their personal needs, wants, and desires, you would be in a better position to influence their thinking. But, how do you determine what type of personality they have? How do you analyze your own personality, so you can use its strengths to influence their personality? That's what this chapter is all about.

PERSONALITY TYPES

A 2003 survey by the Association of Test Publishers showed a significant growth in the use of personality tests by businesses. The most popular of these tests is based on the Myers-Briggs Type Indicators (MBTI). World-renowned psychologists Katherine Cook Briggs and her daughter, Dr. Isabel Briggs Myers began to develop this test during World War II. (The final version of the MBTI test was published in 1962.)

MBTI's enormous appeal stems in part from its simplicity. The questions on the type-indicator test do in fact assess one's personality with a surprising degree of accuracy. But like a miracle diet, some managers expected it to be a quick fix once they discovered what type of personalities they had to deal with.

Personality type is only one piece of the puzzle. You must understand how an individual's personality affects their inspirational and motivational drive to establish goals and their relationships with others to complete the puzzle. You need to know the dominant—as well as the less-dominant—features of your personality, and how your personality interacts with the personalities of others upon whom you rely. Once you're armed with this knowledge, you will be in a much better position to come to terms not only with yourself, but with the people whose personality types and styles are different from yours.

As you proceed through the personality self-discovery process, you will begin to understand why you always seem to be in conflict with a particular colleague, or why your boss doesn't seem to appreciate certain aspects of your work. When you can skillfully inspire, motivate, persuade, and build a synergy in your relationships with others, you will have learned how to unleash the power that's inherent in your personality.

TAKING THE PERSONALITY TEST

You're about to take a personality test that's a shortened version of the original MBTI test. It will help you identify your dominant personality type (i.e., Type One, Two, Three, or Four). It will also help you understand why you think and act the way you do.

It's unlikely that your personality type will prove to be 100 percent of any one of the four types. Most people have a strong affinity for one particular type tinged with influences from the other personality types. If your test results reflect high scores in more than one personality type, you may at first find it difficult to identify your dominant personality type. Don't worry because I'll provide you with insights in the next chapter that will show you how to determine your personality type and style.

Directions
1. Mark the word in each block of four words that most readily comes to your mind.
2. No blank answers are allowed.
3. Strive to choose the words that are most typical of your thoughts and actions.

After you complete the test, I will show you how to determine your personality type, based upon the words that you've selected. You can also try to determine the personality types of others, based on the words you think they would have selected in the same test.

Personality Test

a. Opinionated b. Responsible c. Accepting d. Positive	a. Determined b. Honest c. Content d. Charismatic	a. Productive b. Right c. Positive d. Easy	a. Task-oriented b. People-oriented c. Free of pressure d. Lighthearted
a. Decisive b. Loyal c. Content d. Playful	a. Impatient b. Moody c. Passive d. Impulsive	a. Powerful b. Perfectionist c. Indecisive d. Self-oriented	a. Opinionated b. Nurturing c. Inventive d. Outgoing
a. Calculating b. Self-righteous c. Self-critical d. Disorganized	a. Arrogant b. Concerned c. Stubborn d. Flighty	a. Task-driven b. Sincere c. Diplomatic d. Lively	a. Insensitive b. Judgmental c. Boring d. Undisciplined
a. Action b. Analytical c. Easygoing d. Carefree	a. Demanding b. Unforgiving c. Unmotivated d. Vain	a. Independent b. Dependable c. Even-tempered d. Trusting	a. Always right b. Guilt-prone c. Unenthusiastic d. Uncommitted
a. Critical b. Sensitive c. Shy d. Obnoxious	a. Dominant b. Sympathetic c. Tolerant d. Enthusiastic	a. Confident b. Disciplined c. Pleasant d. Charismatic	a. Logical b. Emotional c. Agreeable d. Popular
a. Assertive b. Reliable c. Kind d. Sociable	a. Responsible b. Idealistic c. Considerate d. Happy	a. Strong-willed b. Respectful c. Patient d. Fun-loving	a. Aggressive b. Depressed c. Ambivalent d. Forgetful
a. Self-serving b. Suspicious c. Unsure d. Naive	a. Argumentative b. Unrealistic c. Lack direction d. No direction	a. Tactless b. Hard to please c. Lazy d. Loud	a. Merciless b. Thoughtful c. Uninvolved d. Show-off
a. Opinionated b. Well-behaved c. Accepting d. Spontaneous	a. Bossy b. Self-critical c. Reluctant d. Teaser	a. Protective b. Concerned c. Supportive d. Optimistic	a. Aggressive b. Caring c. Easygoing d. Playful

Personality Test *(continued)*

a. Recognition	a. Adventure	a. Driven	a. Openly angry
b. Appreciation	b. Security	b. Deliberate	b. Quiet revenge
c. Respect	c. Safety	c. Patient	c. Controlled anger
d. Praise	d. Excitement	d. Spirited	d. Avoid conflicts
a. Intimidating	a. Powerful	a. Determined	a. Direct
b. Careful	b. Deliberate	b. Detail-oriented	b. Creative
c. Unproductive	c. Gentle	c. Good person	c. Adaptable
d. Afraid	d. Optimistic	d. Social person	d. Performer

INTERPRETING YOUR TEST RESULTS

When you took the personality test, you were asked to select from many behavioral words since behavior both expresses and plays a dominant role in shaping a person's personality. Count the number of a, b, c, and d words that you checked off and write the total for each in the table below. The letter next to each personality type (i.e., Type One, Two, Three, or Four) with the greatest total score reflects your dominant personality type.

TYPE ONE (a):	TYPE TWO (b):	TYPE THREE (c):	TYPE FOUR (d):

To show how the scoring works and how to interpret the results, we'll examine a fictitious character named Dan, who was recently promoted into management at a large company. After taking the Personality Test, Dan counts the total number for a, b, c, and d words that he checked off on the test:

TYPE ONE (a):	TYPE TWO (b):	TYPE THREE (c):	TYPE FOUR (d):
5	25	7	3

Dan then enters the results from the test onto a spreadsheet and examines the results. The largest number of words Dan selected was in Type Two (b). From this he concludes that he had a dominant Type Two personality intermixed with some Type One and Three attributes and a few Type Four attributes.

Like Dan, when you discover your true personality type, you will see yourself differently and more accurately. You'll become more aware of your strengths and weaknesses. Don't be discouraged by any of your weaknesses because I'll show you how to overcome your limitations.

THE PERSONALITY TYPES

In this section I'll give you a brief description of the characteristics and attributes that are predominant in each of the four personality types. The next chapter gives you a comprehensive view, complete with an explanation of the inherent strengths and weaknesses in each type.

Type Ones are normally enterprising, outgoing, expansive, and unrestrained individuals. They want things done their own way and can have problems with authoritarian figures who may not allow them to do everything they want to do. They're independent thinkers and can be uncompromising and tenacious. They like to work, and if they're properly motivated, they are highly productive individuals. They want to be knowledgeable in everything they do and actively seek out respect and recognition from others. Type Ones like to be in the driver's seat and will aggressively seek out any leadership position that allows them to climb the corporate ladder and assume more decision-making authority. On the negative side, Type Ones are vulnerable to criticism and can become defensive, fearful, hypersensitive, reluctant, stubborn, or withdrawn if they are subject to criticism. If they don't get their own way about something that matters to them, they can become defiant, irresponsible, unstable, ruthless, or irritable.

Type Twos are extroverted, unreserved thinkers. This personality type is characterized by extroversion; that is, a gregarious and unreserved person who is idealistic, dedicated, and rational. Type Twos are in their best element when people listen to them and when they are appreciated. They'll readily admit to any mistakes they make and will seek out corrective advice in their search to be understood. They look for opportunities to bring happiness to others. Their adaptive feelings for others are realistic, sensible, and practical in most instances. They'll open doors for people, offer rides when someone's car breaks down, and volunteer for charity functions. More than anything else, they want others to love and respect them. Type Twos need to be constantly thanked for any good work that they do and come equipped with a strong sense of integrity. They can be dogmatic, single-minded, intolerant, and cold to others who cross them. If their darker side emerges, they can become demanding, reactive, shallow, and manipulative.

Type Threes need to always feel good about themselves. Although they are amiable people, they exhibit silent stubbornness when they are treated unkindly. They will open up instantly to people who are kind to them, but are not afraid to share words and their feelings with hostile people. They'll do almost anything to avoid confrontations and like to work on teams where confrontations can be neutralized with team awareness. They'll seldom render an opinion unless it is solicited for fear of offending someone. They are calm, controlled, and restrained individuals. Type Threes are seldom likely to be abusive or hostile to others. They can be cold, controlling, unsympathetic, and indecisive if they are confronted with a difficult situation. Their introverted feelings are often reserved and inaccessible. If things aren't going their way, they can become secretive, melancholy, or helpless.

Type Fours are the happiest of all the personality types and consider life to be one big party of which they are the host. They like to be the center of attention wherever they are at and are in constant search of praise. Looking good socially is very important to them. Friendships command a high priority in their lives because popularity answers one of their basic needs. Easily bored, they actively seek adventure and can never sit still for long periods of time. Type Fours are extroverted, realistic, alert, happy, and pleasant. They tend to think of themselves as visionary thinkers and can become passively aggressive, grandiose in their ideas, obsessive exhibitionists, and self-absorbed in their ideas. As perpetual optimists, Type Fours believe they have the world by the tail and will only confide their fears and frustrations to people they trust. If they are not motivated, they can become ineffective, resistant, stubborn procrastinators.

Now, let's return to our fictional character, Dan, who discovers after taking the test that he has a Type Two personality. He considers himself an extroverted thinker and has to admit to himself that he is sometimes too idealistic in his thinking. His feelings for others are realistic and practical; a quality that he feels earns him the respect of everyone he cares about. Dan is intrigued by the fact that the test results show he has some Type One and Type Three personality attributes. Which attributes does he share with people who have Type One and Three personalities?

ESSENTIAL NEEDS

The plumber, the pianist, the football player, the CEO, and everyone else—including Dan—from time to time share a desire to obtain something that they need, regardless of their personality types. Although their personality type and need patterns are independent of one another, they interact with each other. When some event triggers a person's need for something, his personality attributes motivate his behavior in acquiring what he believes he needs.

All of us have complexes of needs that demand satisfaction. These needs are expressed in our personalities. Interpreting these patterns within yourself and others is an important first step in understanding how human motivation works and how to develop meaningful human relationships. There are three essential categories of needs that play an important role in how we manage tasks and develop our relations with others:

Achievement—the need for accomplishment brought about by one's effort,

Dominance—the need for exerting influence over other people, and

Affiliation—the need for developing a close connection or relationship with someone.

You can determine something about your own needs by taking the Assessment of Needs Test on the following page. Read the statements in the table and rate them as needs that you express sometimes or usually. Be objective in your answers, and don't be influenced by what you think your needs should be or by what you think others want them to be. When you're done taking the test:

1. Count the total number of check marks that you made in the Sometimes and Usually columns.
2. List them in the Score row to determine your score for the Achievement, Dominance, and Affiliation need categories.

Assessment of Needs Test

NEED FOR ACHIEVEMENT	SOMETIMES	USUALLY
I like to do the best at whatever task I undertake.		
I like to say that I have done a difficult job well.		
I like to be able to do things better than others.		
I like to do tasks that others recognize require skill.		
I enjoy work as much as play.		
ACHIEVEMENT SCORE		

NEED FOR DOMINANCE	SOMETIMES	USUALLY
I argue with zest for my point of view vs. others' views.		
I can dominate a business situation that interests me.		
I like to be a leader in any organization I am a part of.		
I usually influence others more than they influence me.		
I enjoy a sense of power when I control others' actions.		
DOMINANCE SCORE		

NEED FOR AFFILIATION	SOMETIMES	USUALLY
I like to be loyal to my friends and associates.		
I like to do things for my friends and associates.		
I like to share my feelings with friends and associates.		
I enjoy working with others more than working by myself.		
I talk about controversial issues with congenial people.		
AFFILIATION SCORE		

SCORING YOUR NEEDS ASSESSMENT

A need is considered high if four or five responses were recorded in any one of the three need categories. A score of two to three responses is considered medium, and less than that is considered low. A profile of the needs that are typical of each personality type is shown in the table on the following page.

Profile of Needs by Personality Type

NEEDS	TYPE ONE	TYPE TWO	TYPE THREE	TYPE FOUR
Achievement	High	Medium	Medium	Low
Dominance	High	Medium	High	Low
Affiliation	Low	Medium	High	High

Returning to our example, recall that Dan is interested in finding out what personality attributes he shares with Type Ones and Type Threes. Referring to the needs table and his needs test results, he discovers that he has a "high" need for achievement, a Type One attribute, and a high need for affiliation, a Type Three attribute. A discussion of the three need categories follows:

ACHIEVEMENT

The need for achievement is the need to do one's best, to be successful, and to accomplish tasks that require an effort to complete. How much effort an individual is willing to expend to achieve something she wants is directly related to her motivational level.

You can satisfy achievement needs in different ways: winning an athletic event, working to obtain a material object like a car, or improving your self-esteem by being promoted at work. The need for achievement is usually driven by one's individual desires rather than a collaborative effort with others. For example, you might volunteer for a task that requires the use of your skills and expertise. The fact that if you successfully complete the task, you'll receive a large monetary reward is all you need to become highly motivated to get started without any help from your colleagues.

Leaders with strength in achievement have high personal standards that drive them to constantly seek improvement in their performance and in those that they lead. They're pragmatic and set challenging but attainable goals. A hallmark of achievement is in the desire to continually learn and teach others better ways of doing things.

DOMINANCE

Dominance is the need one has to control the environment, to influence or direct the behavior of others by suggesting, persuading, or commanding them to do something. When it is used aggressively—forcing someone to do something he doesn't want to do, for example—it can create poor morale. If it is used to reward performance, it can be used to motivate people. When you offer a person a reward for completing a specific task that you want done, the reward is a tool to help you dominate the person's behavior.

Some managers show an extreme need for dominance. They'll often say, "Do it because I say so," to flex their dominance. Such managers don't bother explaining the reasons that are behind their order. If subordinates fail to follow their orders unquestioningly, they resort to threats. They seldom delegate authority in order to preserve their tight control over any situation. Accordingly, their performance feedback focuses on what people did wrong rather than what they did right. If the need for dominance in a manager's personality is left unchecked, it will lead to dissonance and the termination of the manager from the organization.

AFFILIATION

Affiliation draws people to you, soliciting their cooperation in getting something done. Affiliation shows itself in group discussions or team settings rather than in working alone. Those with a high need for affiliation have a participative style and form strong bonds with their friends and associates. They like to share their feelings with others and are more comfortable making group decisions. However, people with a high affiliation need may find it difficult to make decisions on their own. If they are given the chance, they will often ask a question like, "What do you think I should do?" before making any decision.

A leader with a keen social awareness can be politically astute, able to detect crucial social networks and read key power relationships. She understands the political forces that are at work in her organization, as well as the guiding values and unspoken rules that operate among the people there. She is comfortable assimilating into the organization's culture and works well with groups to accomplish whatever needs to be done.

DETERMINING YOUR OWN PERSONALITY STYLE

A lot of ground has been covered in this chapter to help you determine your personality type and to develop a profile of your needs. Obviously, no personality tests can provide you with a complete picture of who you are. To help in that, do a self-analysis.

Start by writing a brief autobiography based on what you have learned from these tests. For example, if the test indicated that you have a strong affinity for others, ask yourself what events in your life either support or reject this finding. Your task is to integrate the applicable personal assessments from the tests with your life's experiences to gain an insight into who you are. Throw out test results that you believe don't apply to you.

After you've completed the self-analysis process, you may want to share what you've learned with a trusted friend who knows you well. Get his or her perception of your findings. Does he or she agree or disagree with your self-analysis? Listen carefully to what your friend has to say, even if you disagree. She or he may uncover points that you overlooked.

What steps can you take to leverage the strengths and minimize the weaknesses that are inherent in your personality? What can you do to strengthen your motivational drive?

PUTTING IT ALL TOGETHER

Once you know what your personality type is and understand your need attributes, you can begin to unleash the power in your personality to inspire, motivate, and persuade others. When done consistently, your professional life will substantially improve.

In this chapter you were introduced to the three essential needs—achievement, dominance, and affiliation. You learned that needs influence a leader's perceptions, judgments, and actions. Human behavior is based on a multitude of need patterns. Interpreting your individual patterns is one of the challenges of understanding and shaping your leadership style. Understanding the different needs of others can help you resolve a myriad of people-related problems.

A lot of personality issues were covered in this chapter to assist you in determining your own personality type and style. Once you know and understand the attributes of your personality type, you will be in a better position to lead your followers. In Chapter 4, I cover the attributes of the four personality types in more detail and show you how to inspire, motivate, and persuade each personality type, as you proceed up the leadership ladder.

Getting to Know the Four Personality Types

If you want to win the game, you've got to know what your teammates can do best.

YOU'VE TAKEN THE personality and needs tests in Chapter 3 to determine if you have a Type One, Two, Three, or Four personality. It's now time to meet each of the four personality types. You'll learn how to quickly recognize the personality types of the people who are in your work life, what turns them on and off, and most importantly, how to persuade, motivate, and inspire them. You will also learn about the strengths and weaknesses of each personality type and how you can build on an individual's strengths and help them overcome their weaknesses to your advantage.

MEET THE POWER PLAYER (TYPE ONE)

Kurt loves power and always did whatever he needed to do to get it. He bolted through Stanford's MBA program in less than a year so that he could cruise Wall Street in the fast lane. Kurt skyrocketed through the management ranks of some of the top financial institutions in the country and made a fortune. I met him at an open house where he was celebrating his fortieth birthday. Having achieved so much by age forty, you would assume that Kurt would feel happy and fulfilled. And yet, as the party wore on, I never saw him smile. Despite all of his success, he looked like a man who was restless, disengaged, and looking to get more out of life. I discovered that he had few personal friends, had chalked up two divorces, and was working on his third. One of his friends told me he was not happy unless things were going exactly the way he wanted them to. Kurt is an extreme Type One.

Profile of Type Ones

Type Ones are independent thinkers who want things done their own way. When growing up, if they were allowed to get away with it, they manipulated their parents, brothers, sisters, and friends. As they got older they became more difficult to manage. Because of their manipulative behavior it became more difficult for them to relinquish the power that they established.

Type Ones like to work, are very career oriented, and are subsequently prone to becoming workaholics. If they are properly motivated, they will complete the job or task that's assigned to them. However, they will resist doing anything that doesn't interest them or that they don't believe is important. Type Ones crave approval from others for their intelligence and knowledge about subjects that are important to them.

They want to be respected for their logically oriented minds and will debate any issue that they believe in. They'll seldom get emotionally involved in a discussion and are unmoved by emotional outbursts by others, which they consider displays of weakness. Type Ones like to present the facts as they see them and consider their own opinions to be simply statements of the facts.

44

Type Ones often love to participate in daring sports such as mountain climbing, skiing, and flying. They are creative. You'll often find them building their own homes, restoring vintage sports cars, or similar large-scale activities.

If you can successfully channel Type Ones' energy into work-related projects that motivate them, they'll get the job done in record time. However, they can wear you down with their tenacious and bossy personalities. They're hard to work with because they like to order people around and display little regard for their coworkers' feelings. If a peer challenges them, they can become aggressive and are not afraid to vent their feelings out in public without much tact.

One of the most significant attributes of a Type One's personality is his indifference to personal relationships. Often he is so determined to be productive that he ignores human relations. If this attribute is not corrected, extreme Type Ones will become ruthless egotists who will eliminate anyone who gets in their way.

Type One Strengths

Type Ones are known for their dominant nature, powerful leadership capabilities, and their determination to get things done. They're the movers and shakers in an organization. They pride themselves on being productive, love to set goals with precise completion dates, and like being in leadership positions where they are in control. They'll actively seek out challenging assignments and because of their tenacious nature, are usually successful at whatever they commit to. They like to measure their success in terms of how much they have accomplished, often in monetary terms. Since they are action oriented, they will not allow any problem to get the best of them until they have exhausted every possible remedy to eliminate the problem.

Authority or highly competitive situations rarely intimidate Type Ones. If you need a team leader to tackle what may appear to be an impossible task, select a Type One. They will throw themselves into any assignment that they believe will help them get ahead. They may burn up a couple of their team members in the process, but they'll get the job done. If you seek the advice of a Type One, she'll express herself in a logical manner that's often difficult to refute. She always considers her advice to be right-on and to the point.

Many Type Ones are notably bright individuals and are good decision-makers. Their desire to lead drives them to seek opportunities for advancement. Below is a summary of the strengths inherent in a Type One personality:

- Are creative and logical thinkers, who thrive in competitive situations;
- Thrive on independence and in high-level leadership positions;
- Are committed to productivity and like to contribute productivity-oriented suggestions;
- Communicate their thoughts well, both verbally and in writing;
- Know how to set and complete goals with confidence;
- Are highly disciplined and can make decisions quickly;
- Function well under extreme pressure and are willing to work long hours; and
- Maintain a high self-esteem and know how to keep themselves motivated.

Type One Weaknesses

In spite of their innate self-confidence, Type Ones often suffer from insecurity complexes that stem from their fear of failing to accomplish what they set out to do. To compensate for their insecurity, they seek acceptance, guidance and understanding from others whom they trust. However, they can become so defensive about their own insecurity that they go to great lengths to hide it from others. Don't be surprised to see a Type One abruptly leave a stressful meeting if it threatens his security. If you confront him about it, often he will make an excuse—"I had to use the restroom"—rather than acknowledge his own emotional vulnerability.

Over time, some strong Type Ones convince themselves they have no need for emotion. As a result, they tend to be insensitive to other people's problems. For example, a Type One manager, after learning that one of his key employees' father had died early that morning, called the employee at home to ask him if he would be able to come into the office to complete the proposal that he'd been working on. Type Ones' insensitive feelings toward others explains why they have difficulty maintaining personal relationships.

Extreme Type Ones find it difficult to be intimate or even like other people, one of their greatest disabilities. They can become so focused on their quest for higher productivity that all personal relationships become meaningless to them.

They're highly critical of others and can become very impatient with what they perceive as another person's inadequacy. They will have little sympathy for someone who they believe is impeding progress including employees, peers, management, friends, spouses, and even their own children. They believe that nothing short of efficiency should be tolerated and have no tolerance for people who get in the way.

Although quality is not nearly as important as productivity is to a Type One, they want any job that's important to them done right. They expect results and waste little time informing others of their expectations. If they are in a position of authority at work, they'll often fire people on the spot who, in their judgment, are not productive. Their rigidity and need to hide their own insecurities permeates their personality.

Type Ones believe they are right most of the time. If they're presented with evidence that shows they were wrong, they will brush off their error as a misunderstanding: "She didn't tell me what she really wanted, and that is why my solution to the problem didn't work." They are comfortable with most verbal arguments as long as the confrontation does not threaten their ego. Many Type Ones will spend just as much time and energy arguing over mundane issues, such as how their monthly utility bills should be paid, as they would arguing about how a key project should be funded. Below is a summary of the weaknesses inherent in a Type One personality:

- Are self-serving and consider themselves always right even when they're wrong,
- Will promote turmoil and conflict if it suits their needs to get whatever they want,
- Can be inconsiderate and insensitive to the feelings of others,
- Are quick to be adversely judgmental of others rather than themselves,
- Dislike being told what to do and will challenge anybody who confronts them, and
- Consider work more important than personal relationships.

Motivating Type Ones

In many respects, as a manager you'll have the easiest time motivating Type Ones. They're direct, decisive, and determined, a combination of factors that are essential to success. They are work oriented and focused. However, Type Ones have relatively short attention spans, a quality you need to be aware of when you're attempting to motivate them. Always be direct, brief, and to the point when you're communicating with a Type One. Be prepared to back up anything you say with facts and present your issues in a logical order. If you can offer a Type One any kind of leadership position such as a team lead, you will immediately trigger his motivation button and get his attention.

Type Ones want to control their own lives and they do not like or value anyone who tries to tell them where they should be going or what they should be doing. If you want to motivate a Type One to take on a particular task, offer the assignment as an option for which you're asking their buy-in. As a Type One's manager, if you say, "Susan, I have an assignment for you. Come to my office and I'll give you the specifics," you will irritate the heck out of her. Susan will probably take twice as long to complete the assignment and will bad-mouth you every chance she gets. On the other hand, you might say, "Susan, I need someone with your qualifications to take on a critical assignment for me, which is . . . Do you have any suggestion or recommendations?" Susan is likely to jump at the chance to show off her skills and shine within the organization. The use of power tactics and argumentative confrontations are a waste of time if you are trying to motivate a Type One.

Type Ones benefit from the fact that they limit the amount of emotional material they'll allow in their lives. Once they're motivated, they don't require a great deal of emotional support to perform well. In a team setting, they'll push everyone on the team to be a producer. Type Ones love to set goals. All you need to tell Susan is when you want a job completed. She'll figure out all of the tasks that need to be completed to get it done on time. Here's a brief summary of motivational techniques for Type Ones:

- Offer them rewards and bonuses for their good work.
- Appeal to their desire to be highly productive at whatever they do.
- Applaud them on their goal-setting capabilities.
- Appeal to them in logical rather than emotional terms that show them why the resolution of personal conflicts will help them accomplish their goals.
- Address the main subject first to capture their attention.
- Avoid upsetting them and triggering their insecurities.

MEET THE TEAM PLAYER (TYPE TWO)

Roger is a team player—he always has been, and he always will be. And, he is fast. In high school, I loved watching him take a hockey puck and dart down the rink for a score, making a slew of defenders fall as they chased him. Every time he touched the puck, you knew he was going to do something crazy like give it to one of his teammates just before he was about to shoot for an easy score.

Roger is now twenty-nine. He's liked by almost everybody and does anything he can to help out his friends and associates. I've found myself suggesting to Roger that he pay more attention to his own interests than to the interests of others. He's politely told me to mind my own business.

Profile of Type Twos

Of the four personality types, Type Twos are the most admired by their managers and coworkers. They like to do nice things for others and actively look for opportunities to bring happiness to their associates. They'll likely be the ones you will see holding doors open for friends, offering them rides, and volunteering for charity functions. More than anything, Type Twos want to be appreciated and are willing to sacrifice their career objectives to improve an important personal relationship.

They want people to understand them and will often acknowledge their own inadequacies to others in their attempt to be better understood. They are easily upset when confronted by ridicule that undercuts this need to be understood. Type Twos allow their behavior code to guide them to make the right moral decision on and off the job. They have a strong sense of integrity and would rather lose than win by cheating. They're opinionated because they generally base their opinions on emotion and moral principle rather than logic. Although they try to be logical when making strategic decisions, they can be heavily influenced by the emotional side of their personalities.

On the positive side, Type Twos are sensitive to other people. On the negative side, they can become so emotionally involved in a personal situation that it overpowers their better business judgment. As a result, they are subject to emotional trauma and depression both on and off the job. For example, a Type Two might react to a sudden corporate layoff with an emotional outburst: "I hate this company and everybody who's responsible for this layoff! I resent the fact that they didn't lay me off! How am I going to explain that to my friends who were terminated?"

Shortly after making such a statement, a Type Two may come to his senses and realize that he may have sealed his own fate. He'll quickly deploy damage control measures to neutralize what he's said, apologizing for his outburst and declaring his loyalty to the firm.

In their personal relationships, Type Twos like to be liked, and if they trust you, they will do anything for you. They'll seldom miss an important birthday, wedding, anniversary, or any other special event that means something to anybody they care about. They enjoy companionship and are willing to sacrifice personal gain to save a personal relationship. As a result, they tend to develop lifetime relationships and remain loyal to their friends through good and bad times.

Type Two Strengths

If you walk into a Type Two's office, you may find a sign neatly framed on the wall that says in big, bold letters, "If a job is worth doing, then it's worth doing well." Such a sign would sum up the self-discipline that is an important component of a Type Two's personality. They become highly motivated when they are rewarded and often like to cover their walls with award plaques and pictures. They'll constantly seek out opportunities to refine their many talents and have no problem being thrown into complex projects where they can develop their capabilities. Their self-confidence brings stability to their lives, and their steady, predictable nature means you can depend on them.

They thrive in environments where there is job security and when motivated, will work their hearts out to accomplish whatever someone wants them to do. Type Twos readily accept organizational policies, procedures, and authority since they believe that any organization, whether business or social, requires structure and discipline in order to function properly. They have a strong work ethic, and you will seldom find them wasting time around the water cooler engaging in frivolous, unproductive discussions with others. If they see their coworkers engaged in frivolous activities, they won't openly ridicule them but will privately tell them to get back to work.

Their personalities drive them to participate in life in a steady, orderly fashion. They appreciate intimate relationships and their own creative accomplishments over material things. Type Twos like to be involved in team assignments to solve serious problems and feel comfortable in a situation where they can apply their creative talents. They are motivated when they believe they have a purpose in whatever they are doing.

They'll work for any cause they believe will enhance their human relationships. To accomplish this goal, they'll listen to others before they render their opinion in order to find the best way to meet goals and objectives. They expect the same from others. They will readily adapt to alternative ways of doing something even if it deviates from the way they think things should be done. Type Twos can be the glue that holds an organization and personal relationship together. Here's a summary of the strengths inherent in a Type Two personality:

- Are high achievers with a deep sense of purpose;
- Are stable, dependable, and emotionally solid individuals;
- Are highly disciplined and goal-oriented, with superb follow-through discipline;
- Are analytically oriented individuals, receptive to others' ideas and suggestions;
- Respect authority and work well behind the scenes to support management; and
- Show loyalty to the people they trust and are sensitive to the feelings of others.

Type Two Weaknesses

Type Twos are perfectionists who can become emotionally upset if they feel they're not qualified to accomplish a task that has been assigned to them. As a result, they may have difficulty communicating their expectations and concerns about a project to others.

It can be difficult to determine what their priorities are and how to address their concerns. Even if you discover what a Type Two's expectations are, they may be at such an unrealistic level that they'll be impossible to meet. It's not uncommon to walk away after a conversation scratching your head and wondering; "What was Roger talking about? What does he want to do?"

Type Twos will often watch over their peers who are working with them like mother hens to make sure that they don't make any mistakes. Roger may think this nurturing behavior is welcome by everyone, when in fact many people resent it. It's difficult to convince a Type Two that everyone may not appreciate his good intentions. Roger can be very unforgiving if someone crosses him. For example, if you ask Roger; "Have you ever worked for someone whom you didn't like?" Although all of us have worked for bosses that we didn't appreciate, a Type Two will describe their negative relationship in minute detail and will tell you what they did to get even with them! Resentment is one of their greatest personality weaknesses.

Roger tends to worry about everything, which can make it difficult for him to function in highly stressful work environments. His worrying complex sometimes leads him to feel guilty about almost anything, even if the problem or situation is not his fault. Instead of getting the job done, he'll chastise himself, focusing on emotional rather than rational issues. He can get stuck in ruts where he loses his perspective and often find himself misunderstood. Following is a summary of the weaknesses that are inherent in a Type Two personality:

- Can become highly emotional, smug, and self-righteous;
- Will avoid a high profile in adverse situations that they do not want to be associated with;
- Are rigid in their principles and unwilling to negotiate with people they don't like or respect;
- Expect others to always understand them and to be sensitive toward their feelings;

- Become easily discouraged if they fail to meet their goals and objectives;
- Crave job security and become highly emotional if job insecurity develops; and
- Tend to downplay the capabilities of others relative to their own capabilities.

Motivating Type Twos

Type Twos are highly complex individuals, which can make it difficult to determine how to turn them on and off. They have powerful personality strengths on the one side and debilitating weaknesses on the other. They are overtly sensitive, tense, caring, critical, giving, and unforgiving. They're torn between guilt from unrealistic expectations caused by perfectionist attitude and their expectations of high productivity. Often they're caught between wanting to be involved in a project and their fear of failure. One effective way to motivate Type Twos and to counter their fear of failure is to convince them that failure is the best way to improve whatever they're working on. Remind them that Thomas Edison's experiment with the light bulb failed over 2,000 times before he hit on the right solution and got one to work.

Type Twos suppress their insecurities with self-righteous attitudes and will sometimes go to great lengths to defend how well they believe they are doing on an assignment. Unlike their vocal Type One counterparts, Type Twos remain relatively quiet. They sometimes view the world through suspicious eyes, which influences their pessimistic attitude and unrealistic expectations of perfection. You must recognize and eliminate these unrealistic expectations with a "reality check" before you can successfully motivate a Type Two to accomplish something that is realistic.

Type Twos become resentful and are unforgiving to anyone who crosses them in a business or personal relationship even though they will sometimes blame themselves for having caused the bad relationship. If they are in a leadership position, they'll often blame themselves for the irrational and emotional behavior of others. To help solve this motivational problem, convince them that they can't be responsible for everybody's problems. Here are some suggestions on how to motivate Type Twos:

- Offer a reward for the successful completion of an assignment.
- Reinforce their need for security whenever the opportunity presents itself.
- Limit the risk level of whatever assignment you delegate to them.
- Be sensitive and sincere to excite their motivational drive.
- Promote their creativity and allow them ample time to collect their thoughts on creative ideas.
- Get their full cooperation and earn their trust before placing demands on them.

MEET THE DIPLOMATIC PLAYER (TYPE THREE)

Lydia is a woman of enormous conviction. She has strong opinions about what needs to be done to improve life for everyone. She wants to be a positive force for the people that she cares about. Being the true diplomat that she is, she will take whatever action she can to avoid conflicts and disruptive situations. She's an excellent team player and openly solicits ideas from others. If she likes and trusts you, she will do whatever she can to support you. However, she can be abrasive if she believes that you don't respect her views.

You won't find a long list of goals on Lydia's plate. She'll be the first to tell you that although she has some goals that she wants to accomplish, she will start working on them "whenever she can find the time to fit them in." As a result, it is difficult to keep her motivated for extended periods of time.

Profile of Type Threes

Type Threes like work environments that are free of any hassles because feeling good all the time is very important to them. They become highly motivated when they are treated with thoughtfulness and conversely, will display a silent stubbornness when they are treated unkindly. They are quiet, independent individuals who can become very bullheaded when things don't go their way. People who try to take advantage of a peace-loving Type Three by being too demanding on them will quickly be confronted with a wall of passive resistance. Type Threes do not like to be controlled and are openly hostile to anybody they believe does not respect them. They're tougher than people sometimes take them for and can maintain a powerful resistance to a course of which they disapprove.

They like doing things their own way and will not place demands on others to help them; in the same way, they resent people who place demands on them. They'll often comply with unreasonable or impossible demands just to keep the peace in an organization. They respond well to suggestions and are open to work-related recommendations that will help resolve problems or improve an overall situation. Type Threes make excellent team members if they are encouraged to openly communicate their ideas. However, if you do not solicit comments from them, they will say little and seldom offer an opinion.

They appear to approach life in an easy, self-controlled manner that can lead one to believe they're at peace with themselves. In reality, Type Threes often have hidden feelings that can be influenced by fear, timidity, or personal inadequacy. For this reason, Type Threes are more difficult to motivate than the other personality types.

If left alone, Type Threes will rarely assume any independence or leadership on their own. They often make others the core of their existence so that they do not have to develop their own sense of purpose or direction. In their most extreme form, they can become so attached to one person or a group of people that they will avoid developing outside interests or making commitments that would separate them from that association. Transferring a close associate of a Type Three to another location could have a devastating effect on them. The next day, their manager may find on her desk the Type Three's transfer request to the same location.

Type Three Strengths

Type Threes like to accommodate others as they move through their lives. Their gentle nature and superb use of diplomacy wins them many loyal friends and associates. They can be a blend of the best from all of the personality types. Like water in a mountain stream, they can flow around problems and rocks that get in their way. They will generally take the path of least resistance if they can find it.

They are fully capable of accepting other people's opinions, are more than willing to learn from others, and will encourage people to work together. Like chameleons, they can adapt and blend in with everyone because of their enviably balanced personality. They know how to keep the problems of life in the right perspective; they are patient, tolerant, and have much to give if you know how to motivate them.

Type Threes like to be in agreement with almost everyone they meet including people they don't like. They're fully capable of adopting positive personality attributes from the other personalities once they become convinced that those attributes can better serve their needs.

Because of their tolerant expectations, people from other personality types will actively seek them out for their advice. Here's a summary of the strengths that are inherent in a Type Three personality:

- Have quiet, reflective, peaceful personalities that blend into all situations;
- Are comfortable with most people;
- Communicate well with others, are receptive to their ideas, and are superb listeners;
- Recognize the value of setting goals and objectives to achieve what they want out of life;
- Remain calm under pressure and can function well in crisis situations; and
- Work well in bureaucratic environments and respect the leadership qualities of others.

Type Three Weaknesses

Type Threes are dominated by self-doubt and must constantly be stroked to reinforce their need to be accepted. Because of their fear of not being accepted, they don't trust others freely and will not disclose their true feelings until they trust you. They're also dreamers. You'll often find them staring off into space thinking about something other than what they should be doing. This unproductive personality attribute can cause them to miss timely assignments and produce a minimum amount of work. Because of their daydreaming, they sometimes lack real world direction and can be the least self-motivated of all the personality types.

They are reluctant to set goals and will wait until they can establish goals they believe in and can commit to—even if that means working without direction for a lengthy time. They are often unwilling to set goals for fear that if their goals are not met, they will face rejection from their peers. If they do find a goal they like, they may say something like, "I've finally seen the light at the end of the tunnel. I now know what I want to do!" They'll remain committed to their goals until they see a better light, a pattern that may cause them to constantly change their goals rather than complete the ones they originally set out to accomplish.

Type Threes can be lazy and as a result, are the first to miss out on opportunities. They don't like change since they perceive change as another word for work rather than an opportunity. These flaws make Type Threes a challenge to lead and motivate. They'll move sluggishly throughout their job assignments with no desire to set any records. "Everything comes to he who waits" is one of their favorite mottoes. However, the effective use of emotional threats can frighten them into short-term bursts of productivity. They rely on others rather than themselves to hand them opportunities, are vulnerable to wasting time, and can become dull due to their reluctance to change.

Type Threes rarely seek out leadership positions since they are more comfortable in subordinate roles. They don't like to make decisions that could be wrong and prefer to leave the decision-making responsibility to someone else. Below is a summary of the weaknesses that are inherent in a Type Three personality:

- Can become bored and detached from their job or assignment;
- Are unsure of themselves, resist making commitments, and often take the passive approach to anything they do;
- Show ambivalence about setting goals that require real commitment and hard work;

- Lack consistency in setting goals and measuring their accomplishments;
- Fear confrontations and therefore can be easily manipulated if they are threatened with a confrontation;
- Are sometimes dishonest about what they want;
- Would rather take an inactive than an active role to resolving problems; and
- Are not high producers and are difficult to motivate for extended periods of time.

MOTIVATING TYPE THREES

Type Threes can become overwhelmed by problems, even the ones they can't control. A sudden conflict in the world can cause them to lose their focus on what needs to be done at work or in their personal lives. Motivate a Type Three by patiently listening to their concerns. Then firmly remind them about what needs to get done today, regardless of what's happening in the real world or in their fantasy world, a delay tactic that Type Threes tend to employ. You'll be successful at motivating Type Threes if you can earn their trust and get them to express themselves to you.

Because of their personal insecurities, they are reluctant to set and pursue goals. In many cases, if they have goals, they have difficulty determining what goal to pursue first. As a manager, you should set and prioritize goals for your Type Three employees. The key to your success at motivating a Type Three is to solicit their commitment to the goals you set. If the employee doesn't have firmly established goals, she is next to impossible to motivate. Motivational techniques for Type Threes include:

- Be sensitive but firm when communicating to Type Threes.

- Listen carefully to what they have to say and look for nonverbal clues of expression that indicate they are sincere in what they say.
- Foster their need to be treated as individuals and provide a work structure that's comfortable for them to work in.
- Constantly offer ideas for goals and present them with opportunities to participate in goal-oriented assignments with others.
- Monitor their progress toward completing assigned goals and be prepared to initiate corrective action if they start to miss goal-related completion dates.

MEET THE PARTY PLAYER (TYPE FOUR)

Dale changes people the moment he walks into a room where his associates are gathered. If the people in the room weren't smiling before he entered, they are as soon as they see him, shake his hand, and pat him on the back. He has an ability to excite and attract people to his side, making them anxious to listen to whatever he has to say.

To Dale, life is one big party to be taken in and enjoyed to its fullest, and he is the hit of the party. He'll tell you, "Yeah, you have got to work if you want to pay your bills, but just don't take it too seriously." When someone asks, "What about your career goals and objectives?" he answers with a smile, "What are goals and objectives? If they are something that's fun to work on, then I'll consider doing them."

Dale is an outstanding example of the Type Four employee. In general, he likes to be in agreement and harmony with everyone. To that end, he is obedient and readily accepts the prevailing standards in his effort to avoid any confrontations, which he will go to great lengths to do.

Profile of Type Fours

Type Fours love to have fun at everything they do and consider life to be one big party. Unlike Type Threes, they're extroverted with realistic, alert, jolly, and pleasant personalities. They consider themselves visionary thinkers and can become grandiose when expressing their ideas. They can become obsessive exhibitionists when communicating to people that they're trying to impress. They're also perpetual optimists.

Type Fours believe they have the world by the tail and will only confide their fears and frustrations to their closest friends. They need to know that they are appreciated and have full approval on everything they do from the people that they trust. They like to be the center of attention and are constantly searching for praise to reinforce their need to feel good. Being socially prominent in any situation is very important to them. Friendships command a high priority in their lives because popularity answers one of their basic needs.

Easily bored, they actively seek adventure and can never sit still for long periods of time. Strategic planning is not their forte. They are reluctant to set goals that require a lot of work unless they are certain of the benefits they'll realize when they meet specific goals. They'll often act as though nothing bothers them. Because of their nonchalant attitude, you may think they don't care about anything. However, nothing could be further from the truth: their fear is that they will lose their popularity. For this reason, they need a great deal of management attention.

Type Four Strengths

Type Fours are impetuous by nature and love adventure, such as traveling to exciting places where experiences are more apt to be spontaneous. They're not afraid to make tough decisions and constantly look for opportunities that offer excitement. Because of their enthusiasm for life, people like to be around Type Fours because they are bent on enjoying life even when they're working hard under pressure.

They're great generalists who rarely become bogged down with details or emotional problems. Although they are as vulnerable to adverse experiences as any of the other personality types, they have a strong yearning for freedom and will quickly move away from individual confrontations. For example, they will avoid listening to a peer's adverse gossip unless the colleague can provide proof of what they're talking about.

They always believe that the best in life is yet to come, which reinforces their self-confidence. Type Fours find it easy to relate to people of all ages and walks of life. They have the most engaging communication style of all the personality types and can draw people to themselves as if they were a magnet. You'll always find people gathered around them at company Christmas parties or social gatherings. They like to conduct business charismatically and can be good motivators both for themselves and for others.

Type Fours actively promote the good in others and are willing to ignore their own limitations. They're constantly seeking out new ideas and relationships that will help them experience life to its fullest. In the process, they express themselves candidly, and inspire others to do the same. They freely spread a contagious spirit of friendship wherever they go. They are the people connectors and the social glue that holds people and organizations together. Below is a summary of the strengths that are inherent in a Type Four personality:

- Are highly optimistic, very self-confident, and easily accept the opinions of others;
- Perceive life as an experience to be enjoyed and readily volunteer for challenging assignments;

- Think out of the box with excellent communication skills and are willing to compromise in order to get things done;
- Show energy if they are involved with groups such as work teams and are willing to accept guidance from others;
- Demand action from others on key projects that are important to them; and
- Have a high energy level and inspire others to cooperate in team settings.

Type Four Weaknesses

Of all the personality types, Type Fours are the most apt to do superficial work as they bolt through life focused on having fun. They frequently fail to develop any meaningful depth in a job because their focus is elsewhere. One of their most serious limitations is their inability to make long-term commitments. They'll start more projects than any of the other personality types and complete the least, since they don't like to make commitments that tax their limited capacity for work. Type Fours are often reluctant to take on the responsibility for setting up their own self-improvement programs, believing that is someone else's responsibility. They're not opposed to self-improvement as long as it doesn't require a lot of effort on their part.

Getting to know one's self is a difficult and painful task for anyone since it involves painfully reviewing all of one's personality strengths and weaknesses. Although Type Fours may start the process, they will most likely end it before they get very far. Having fun always has a higher priority with Type Fours.

Although Type Fours will give you the positive signs you think you need to get them on a goal-oriented track, getting them to stay on the track is another matter, and keeping them motivated is a challenge. They're not comfortable with the pressures that are associated with responsibility. If things are not going their way, they will blame others. It's one of the many techniques they employ to avoid taking on responsibility. Their flighty disposition makes them constantly looking for something new and exciting to do.

Although a Type Four will reluctantly accept a management position, you won't find many of them in upper management. Type Fours aren't interested in power positions, and even if they were, most do not have the discipline to use power. None of the other personality types are as naive or as trusting as Type Fours. They're easily fooled and are often taken advantage of by the other more calculating personality types. They trust everybody and as a result, can become devastated by broken commitments. Here's a summary of the weaknesses that are inherent in a Type Four's personality:

- Can only handle stress for short periods of time;
- Are self-centered, irresponsible, and unreliable when working on anything that doesn't interest them;
- Talk a lot about what they are going to do with little attention to actually getting anything done;
- Don't like to commit to long-term goals that require serious work to complete;
- Will freely interrupt a serious conversation with irrelevant remarks; and
- Often unwilling to dedicate themselves to causes unless the tasks are fun to work on.

MOTIVATING TYPE FOURS

Type Fours are spontaneous. They are always ready to take on whatever fun opportunities come their way. I've found them wearing T-shirts with slogans like "Work is the Curse of the Party

Man." Their inherent desire to have fun makes it difficult to motivate them to do anything they don't want to do. Any assignment you give them that includes a "fun-related" reward for its successful completion will motivate a Type Four. Award dinner parties, letters of recognition, and group acknowledgments are some of the best ways to reward Type Fours. They love to receive applause from others for their talents.

Some Type Fours want to modify their behavior, but change demands a commitment from them that they're reluctant to make. If you can convince them that the effort they need to implement a change will earn them applause from others, you can raise their motivational level several notches. Here are some suggestions about motivating Type Fours:

- Always be positive with Type Fours. Tell them what a great job they're doing.
- Plan recognition events for completing well-defined goals.
- Allow Type Fours to verbally express themselves and listen carefully to what they say to get clues on what you can do to motivate them.
- Don't be too serious or intense when criticizing Type Fours or it will be difficult to motivate them to do anything.
- Schedule regular follow-up sessions to make sure they're meeting their commitments and are still motivated.

MIXED PERSONALITIES

Remember we said in Chapter 2 that most of us are not just one personality type; we have mixed personalities to varying degrees. Very few people (1 out of 10,000) who take my personality test score 100 percent in any one of the four personality types. If you felt you were unable to establish a personality type that fits you

Needs & Wants Attributes of the Personality Types

TYPE	NEEDS/WANTS	STRENGTHS	WEAKNESSES
TYPE ONE Power Players	They need respect and approval from their peers for everything they do. They want to do everything right.	They are committed to hard work, goals, and high levels of productivity. They want to be in leadership positions and demand high work standards from others.	They can become highly irritable if anyone challenges their beliefs that, to them, are always right. They are very impetuous individuals.
TYPE TWO Team Players	They need appreciation and endorsement from their peers for everything they do. They want their feelings to be understood.	They are high integrity individuals who like people and will help them achieve a quality focus. They demand honesty from anyone that they are associated with.	They can become self-righteous and highly judgmental of others who don't meet their high standards. They are easily depressed if someone judges them.
TYPE THREE Diplomatic Players	They need peer support and help in everything they do. They want to be independent and allowed to do their own thing.	They are patient with people and will solicit their cooperation and support in anything they do. They are excellent communicators and respect authority.	They can become very insecure if things aren't going their way. They are reluctant to set difficult goals for fear that they may not meet them.
TYPE FOUR Party Players	They need to feel like they are popular with everyone they care about. They want to be involved in opportunities that are exciting to them.	They are optimists and will go out of their way to help anybody achieve whatever they want. They demand trust in all of their relationships.	They can become rebellious if they are involved in a task that is not fun or rewarding for them. Although they appreciate goals, they don't like to set them for themselves.

or those whom you manage, don't be too concerned. It simply means that the characteristics of your personality and those of your direct reports are harder to pin down. The table on the facing page summarizes the needs and want attributes of the four personality types.

PUTTING IT ALL TOGETHER

Any strategy you develop to become a proactive leader requires that you know how to recognize and interact effectively with the four different personality types. Knowledge of the personality types—knowing which you are and which describe those you manage—will help you come to terms with people whose styles are different from yours. Each personality type brings with it a unique set of strengths and weaknesses. Learn what you can about each of the personality types and develop an appreciation for the unique strengths and limitations of each type. Whether you are talking to an employee or trying to develop a relationship with a peer or superior, your ability to recognize, understand, and leverage to your advantage the personality attributes of whomever you are dealing with will serve you well throughout your career. By studying all of the personality types, you can strengthen the inherent limitations of your own personality type, which will significantly improve your leadership capabilities. In the process, develop the strengths of your personality and work on overcoming the weaker part of your psyche.

Quality Traits of the Four Personality Type

	TYPE 1	TYPE 2	TYPE 3	TYPE 4
COMMITMENT	Direct	Creative	Adaptable	Spontaneous
COMMUNICATION	Driven	Deliberate	Patient	Spirited
COMPETENCE	Determined	Self-righteous	Content	Uncommitted

CHAPTER 5

Developing an Empowered Personality

Your personality is the most powerful personal weapon you've got if you know how to use it.

WESTERN ARTIST FREDERICK Remington had an inspiration that empowered his personality. In 1885, he went to Tombstone, Arizona, to draw his impression of a cattle drive that was going to pass through the center of town. On the morning of the drive, he was sitting on a bench that overlooked the historic OK Corral talking with a friend. His friend asked if he would draw a sketch of him while he was waiting. Remington immediately reached into the trash can next to him and removed a piece of paper. His friend replied, "That's not sketching paper, it's ordinary wrapping paper. You can't draw on that!" Not wanting to lose his spark of inspiration for the sketch, Remington held the wrapping paper up and said, "Nothing is ordinary if you know how to use it." On that ordinary piece of wrapping paper, Remington made two sketches that would later be worth over fifty thousand dollars. An empowered person knows how to make something out of nothing.

THE ART OF EMPOWERMENT

Have you ever seen a motivational speaker work a group of people up into a state of cheering, yelling, and arm-waving hysteria? The really good ones brim over with self-confidence as they assure their audience that if people really believe they're empowered, they can accomplish anything. Simply defined, empowerment is the ability to influence others.

Inspirational speakers use their empowerment to play on our emotions. They are experts at getting our pulse pounding and our adrenaline racing, which is why people go to their speeches. However, they are useless if you yourself don't want to be empowered. As long as the presentation lasts you may be caught up in the excitement. Fifteen minutes after the seminar is over and you head back into the real world, you'll return to normality. That's precisely where the problem lies.

As a leader, you need to find another way to keep yourself empowered day after day. If you are empowered, you will influence others to reach their highest levels of personal and professional achievement. No matter how hard you work, no matter how engaging your personality may be, if you are unable to motivate others through an empowered personality you won't make it as a leader. In this chapter you'll learn how to empower your personality and persuade others to help you achieve your goals. Always remember that your personality is the most powerful motivational and persuasive tool that you've got in your arsenal—if you know how to empower it.

Although some elements of your personality are innate features that you're born with, as you mature, your personality is also shaped by your ability to commit and communicate with competence. These three qualities—commitment, communication, and competence—help define not only who you are but also how you make positive or negative connections with others. You develop those abilities over the years by personal design, and they become a solid part of your personality. Let's review the three personality qualities to see how they affect each of the personality types and what you can do empower them in yourself.

EMPOWERING YOUR COMMITMENT

Commitment can take on several different forms within your personality. When you're committed, you establish value-linked goals that point toward where you want to go. Values are the ideas and beliefs you hold to be important. They're the underlying principles that determine how you will set or commit your priorities to reach your goals. Values help you fulfill your ambitions in both your business and personal life.

The pursuit of goals must be meaningful to the individual working on them. They're essential to the motivational process since goals provide the rewards needed to maintain motivation. Every goal you set must be based on ideas and beliefs that you hold to be important. They're the underlying principles that determine how you will set your priorities to reach your goals.

Use those goals as the channel markers to make sure you stay on the right leadership course, to help you fulfill your ambitions in both your business and personal life. Commit to goals you believe are good for you, goals that have perceived values for you and your constituents.

You should not commit to a goal unless you believe it is attainable. Most people, no matter how important and value-focused a goal may be to them, won't go after it unless they believe that they have a good chance of obtaining it. For example, you may fantasize about becoming the company's president, but you won't do anything about it if you believe that your education is inadequate to reach that goal.

In the work environment, Type Ones and Threes like to commit to tasks that support the accomplishment of their goals. Type Twos and Fours are more concerned about their own creativity than they are about completing specific goals. As a result, they are less interested in committing to anything that could disrupt their creative thinking. Although Type Twos will set some goals, they will put restrictions on the complexity of the goals they set to help minimize any disappointment if they don't meet their objectives.

Type Fours will set goals if they are exciting to work on or if they are forced by someone else, such as their boss. The moment they're bored by a goal, they'll stop working if they have a choice.

Type Ones tend to rely too much on goals to meet their motivational objectives and would be well advised to adopt some of the Type Two creative characteristics into their thinking. Conversely, Type Twos should look at acquiring Type Ones' committed focus on goals to help them minimize their fear of not completing their goals. Type Threes know how to set goals, but don't like to work on them. They need to concentrate on setting goals that are important to them and to establish aggressive time frames to complete each goal. Type Four personalities need to go back to the basics to learn what goal setting is all about and why goals are important to the motivational process.

There are three primary ways to empower your ability to commit.

Commit from the Heart

The world has never had a leader who wasn't committed. True commitment inspires people and persuades them to follow you. When a leader commits to something that's important to his constituents, it shows them that he has conviction. Employees will follow a leader who commits from the heart.

Committing from the heart—what exactly does that mean? It means making a commitment based on one's beliefs, feelings, and inclinations. The ability to commit from the heart is what separates managers from great leaders. If you want to be an exemplary leader, look into your heart to see if you're ready to commit. Ask yourself, what are the three most important things in your life that you are willing to commit to? If it came down to it, what would happen if you failed to meet those commitments? Other than yourself, who would also suffer because of your failure? Spend some time alone meditating on your thoughts. Then sit back and see if your "real time" actions today are matching what you have committed to do for yourself and others.

Commit to Action

Everybody is filled with good intentions to commit. Walk into any setting where your employees are assembled and ask them to commit. Many will say, "As soon as I get the time, I'm going to do it . . .", "I'm under a lot of pressure just now . . .", "I've got a big project coming up, but after that . . ." The list goes on.

The only real measure of commitment is action. When you make a serious commitment, you had better accompany it with an action plan that's complete with the steps you'll take to meet your commitment, and of course planned start and completion dates for each step. If you don't have an action plan in place, then you're not ready to make a commitment. A clear, step-by-step action plan will persuade your employees you've planned to accomplish your goals, and they'll be much more ready to follow you down that road.

Commit to Win

Winning isn't everything, it is the *only* thing. You can't win anything if you're not willing to commit to something. Of course, the reverse is true. If you never commit to anything, you will never lose. Winners are leaders who are not afraid to lose.

As a leader, when you make a commitment, you will face many obstacles and lots of opposition along the way. There will be times when your commitment to see something through is the only thing that carries you forward. Always commit to win and you will be a winner. And the power of your empowered personality will take others along with you.

EMPOWERING YOUR COMMUNICATION

Have you ever caught yourself thinking, "That idiot doesn't know what I'm trying to tell him. How am I ever going to persuade him to accept my idea?" In order to persuade anybody to do what you want, you have to be an effective communicator. Before I talk about what it takes to empower your communication capabilities, let's first make a clear distinction between persuasion and manipulation. Although many people think that persuasion is just a kinder word for manipulation, there's a huge difference between the two.

Manipulation is using communication to force a person to do something that fulfills your needs, whether or not it's in the best interests of the other person. Persuasion is the art of guiding someone through a logical progression of thoughts so that he can arrive at a conclusion that complements your views and is also in his own best interest. In essence, persuasion enables the other person to understand what you are saying, what you are feeling, and consequently motivates him to do what you believe is in his best interests.

For example, a manager can apply manipulative tactics when she tells a subordinate, "Here's a task I want you to do. Don't ask any questions. Just do it and you might get a reward," though in fact she has no intention of ever providing a reward. Or, she could apply persuasive tactics like, "Here's a task I'd like you to do. Before you get started, let's first discuss why the successful completion is important to our organization and your future." Leaders persuade with meaningful hooks and promises. Bad managers manipulate with force and false promises. There are three primary communication hooks—personal, question, and attention hooks—that you can use to persuade people to do what you want them to do.

Personal Hooks

The personal hook is one that gets an individual's attention because of the personal value she or he places on it. It is therefore one of most effective hooks you can use. I encountered a personal hook when I was attending army boot camp and was talking to my buddy while one of the sergeants was conducting a class on land mines. The sergeant interrupted our conversation and said, "You better listen to what I'm telling you, boy, because it could save your life." From that point on, I was all ears. He had persuaded me with a personal hook (i.e., my life) to listen.

In the business world, you're constantly challenged to get people to listen to you. The sergeant used my life as a personal hook to persuade me, an impatient Type One, to listen to what he had to say. Personal hooks also work well on people-oriented Type Twos, safety-conscious Type Threes, and charismatic Type Fours.

Name-dropping, which is a subset of personal hooks, can be another effective means of getting the attention of Type One power players and Type Two team players.

Suppose you're trying to get an appointment with a vice president who can influence your promotional opportunities. She doesn't know you from Adam. One of the guys in your network knows her well and recommended that you meet with her. You say, "A mutual associate of ours, Dave Rye, suggested that I give you a call and set up a half hour meeting with you. Would 10 A.M. tomorrow work for you?" You've persuaded her by using the power of someone else's name.

Question Hooks

The purpose of the question hook is to take the listener's mind off whatever he was doing before you asked the question and to provide you with information you can use to persuade her to do something when they answer your question.

If you want to get someone's attention by using the question hook, the question must be very specific so that the listener must think carefully before they respond. "What do you think about my idea to create this new product?" is a classic example of an open-ended question hook. When you listen to his response, take information from it that could help you persuade him. Suppose he says, "It's a great product but quite frankly, we are having a tough time figuring out how we're going to introduce it." You just hit pay dirt. "I've got a great product introduction idea for you to consider," you reply. "Would you care to hear about it?"

"Do you agree with my product introduction idea?" is an example of a closed-ended question hook. It requires the recipient to provide you with a "yes" or "no" response. If you get a "yes" response, you may be on your way. If you're given a "no" response, you may have to follow up with an open-ended question to find out what the objections might be.

Attention Hooks

Here's an example of an attention hook statement. You walk into your boss's office for your appointed meeting, shut the door, and say, "If we don't take some immediate action now, we are going to lose our largest account. I have several ideas that will prevent that from happening." In one attention hook statement, you have focused your boss's attention on the problem and persuaded him to learn about your solution.

This sort of strong, direct approach works well with Type One and Type Four personalities. A more subtle approach might be in order if you're addressing a more analytical Type Two or Type Three boss. For example you might start off with; "I have carefully analyzed the cause of the problem that we have with our largest customer and have concluded . . ." All you need to say to a trusting Type Four boss is, "Do you want me to fix the problem we're having with our largest customer?" Eager to avoid any conflicting situations, your Type Four boss will gratefully give you the high sign.

The three hooks, when used in combination, can be powerful tools in persuading someone to do something you want them to do. Jane Fonda used all three hooks in her fitness video commercials. They went something like this: "Hi, I'm Jane Fonda and I have an important message for you (personal hook). Are you one of the 50 million Americans who try to lose weight each year (question hook)? Diets simply don't work, as you'll learn when you order my tape (attention hook)." That fifteen-second commercial persuaded millions of people to buy Fonda's fitness video. Your effective use of hooks when you initiate a conversation will get your listener to focus on what you have to say and get what you want.

In summary, create an opening to your presentation using all three hooks whenever possible. Identify all of the benefits of your idea and how it fulfills the needs of your listeners. Focus on your listener's two greatest internal motivating factors: his desire for gain and his fear of loss. List every possible objection your listener could pose to your idea and state how you will overcome each objection on your list.

EMPOWERING YOUR COMPETENCE

It's a rough road to the top, which is why many "would be" leaders never make it. It is where the best of the best go. That brings us to the John Elway story. He was one of the best quarterbacks to play in professional football for the Denver Broncos (1983–1998). People who know him say he is a natural at empowering his inner competence to accomplish incredible mental and physical feats. According to his former coach, Bill Nash, "I don't think there's a guy equal to him physically. Yet that alone didn't make him great. The real key to John's success was his ability to use his desire for competence to drive his self-discipline. He worked and prepared day in and day out unlike any one player I have ever seen or coached. And, he inspired every member of our team to acquire a level of self-competence that they never thought was possible. He was our team's leader."

Empowered competence refers to a leader's ability to get things done. To enlist in a common cause, people must believe that their leader has the competence to guide them to where they want to go. If they doubt their leader's abilities, they are unlikely to join in the crusade. There are three elements you can apply to empower your competence—drive, discipline, and direction.

Drive

Your drive is your desire to get things done. Drive is closely tied to your ability to perform at an expected level to accomplish your goals. It's been widely established that the average human being only uses about 20 percent of his innate capabilities. It takes energy to apply capabilities. That energy comes in the form of your drive.

Type Ones are driven to accomplish whatever they want out of life. They often believe that their capabilities are unlimited. This can frustrate them if they fail to meet a goal that is beyond their capabilities. Conversely, Type Twos and Threes are very deliberate when assessing their drive to accomplish anything. Spirited Type Fours will often commit themselves to anything without taking the time to consider if they have the necessary qualifications. It's essential for all four types to conduct an honest assessment of their capabilities before they commit to a goal.

Discipline

Discipline means learning to manage yourself. Management used to mean getting things done through others. Today, breakout leaders know that the tougher challenge is to manage themselves. Unlocking your own untapped capabilities and setting subsequent high standards demands that you carefully manage your thoughts, ideas, and energy to accomplish what you set out to do. If you do that, your direct reports will be eager to follow you.

Type Ones are direct, driven, and determined in everything they do. This can cause problems in their relationships with others who don't live up to their expectations. Type Twos like to be creative and deliberate on whatever they work on. They tend to be self-righteous and will challenge an assignment given to them before they will accept it. Type Threes are adaptable in most work environment and demonstrate patience and appreciation for their coworkers. Type Fours are spirited, spontaneous thinkers and doers. The do not have a lot of patience. When they find something that works for them and that they like, they will latch on to it.

Direction

Once you have the drive and discipline to accomplish your goals, you must create a clear and decisive direction and the reasons for taking it. For example, let's assume you decide to get yourself promoted. Review this choice. Does the challenge of getting yourself promoted really turn you on? Is it something that you really want to do? If your answer is "no," then you'll lack the motivation to get yourself promoted.

If you want that promotion, watch what others have done to get ahead so that you can learn from their techniques. Use that to create a road map, with step-by-step goals that will get you to your destination. Work at becoming the best you can be (i.e., most competent) at whatever you want to do. After you become the best there is, figure out a way to get even better. A true leader knows that self-complacency is his worst enemy.

Type Ones carefully calculate the precise direction they want to take to get what they want. Self-righteous Type Twos justify to themselves and others the direction they are about to take before they actually take it. Type Threes are self-critical about all of the options they are considering. They will confide in as many people as they can find to help them make the right decision. Setting a decisive direction can be a frustrating experience for a Type Four, since they tend to be disorganized.

PUTTING IT ALL TOGETHER

Commitment, communication, and competence are three essential components of the leadership empowerment process. Every great leader has tweaked each component to augment the attributes of her or his personality. Who is the one business leader you admire most? Did the leader you chose have a personality with a high level of integrity behind every commitment she or he made? Did that leader communicate to you with clarity and display the highest level of competence possible? You should work to develop an empowered personality that is reinforced by your commitment, communication, and competence. In this way, you'll become the kind of leader others admire.

PART II

Leading Others

LEADERSHIP IS NOT a solo act that wins the game—it requires a team effort. Leaders understand that to create a climate of winning collaboration they need to determine what their team needs are and how to motivate their team around common goals that are reinforced by strong relationships between teammates. They have to know how to coach each of their team members to get extraordinary things done and win the game.

Goal Attributes of the Personality Types

TYPE ONE	They are committed to goals and achieving high levels of productivity to get them where they want to go.
TYPE TWO	They are high integrity individuals who set goals that will help them achieve their quality focus on everything they do.
TYPE THREE	They will pursue goals if they have the cooperation and support of the people that they need to help them achieve their goals.
TYPE FOUR	They are optimists and will pursue goals to achieve whatever they want as long as are they are relatively easy to achieve.

CHAPTER 6

Turning On with Goals

A goal is like a ship's rudder. Turn it in the right direction and it will take you to wherever you want to go in life.

THE HUMAN ABILITY to set goals in order to get whatever we want out of life is an amazing thing. Newspapers and magazines are filled with stories about people who have triumphed against unbelievable odds. Lance Armstrong is an example of a person who set seemingly impossible goals to survive terminal cancer and win the Tour de France bike race. He won the bike race not once, but seven times in a row, and conquered cancer.

In addition to helping us create self-awareness, imagination, and purpose, goals are essential to sustain high levels of motivation. You can achieve short-term increases in productivity and motivation when threat factors like fear or intimidation are applied, but you can only achieve sustained levels of motivation by constantly working to achieve goals that are supported by your own inspiration. Finally, goals are necessary for good team work, giving the team a common set of objectives and making sure everyone knows what she or he is doing and why.

This chapter will show you how to set and achieve meaningful goals first for yourself and then for your team members in a variety of different settings. You'll develop a better understanding of the personality issues that are behind the problems that goals are often set up to resolve. While I can't discuss problems that are identical to the exact ones you face, I can present real-life issues that may be very similar. In this chapter I'll show you how you can use the attributes of your personality and the personality attributes of others to assure you and your team meet your goals and objectives.

GETTING STARTED

If you don't have precise, clearly defined goals, you will never make it to your objective. You'll be like an airplane without a rudder drifting in the clouds rather than heading toward a specific destination you've marked on a map. The story of Eddie Rickenbacker offers a classic example of a man who knew exactly where he was flying. As a young man, he loved to set seemingly impossible goals for himself. In 1914, he set the world automobile speed record at Daytona just before he was sent off to fight in World War I. He was credited with scoring the highest number of aerial combat victories against the Germans in the war and was awarded the Medal of Honor.

Rickenbacker returned to work in the automobile industry after the war, first with his own company and later with the Cadillac Motor Car Company. In 1933, he joined Eastern Air Lines as their president. At this time airlines existed only because they were subsidized by the government. Rickenbacker thought they should be self-sufficient, a goal he set for the company. He completely changed the way Eastern did business. Within two years, the company was profitable, a first in aviation history. He retired as chairman of Eastern's board in 1963. When he died ten years later, his son, William. wrote, "He had a motto I've heard a thousand times: 'I'll fight like a wildcat to meet any goal I set out to accomplish.' My father was one of the best wildcats I ever knew."

Unfortunately, it is easy for people to rattle off a set of goals toward which they are purportedly working. Words are cheap. For every goal that actually gets completed, there are a million that never got started. Action speaks louder than words. Bill Gates knew that when he stated, "The future drives the goals we set for the present!" When he was nineteen, he saw the future in a little computer program called DOS. Mighty IBM didn't, and as Paul Harvey would say, "You know the rest of the story." Gates methodically established goals for his company, Microsoft, and you can rest assured that he's following this same plan today.

Setting Goals

Setting goals is like laying the bricks that will form the foundation of your career and pave your way to a prosperous future. Since it's your future, why not think big? Everybody else who has gotten anywhere consistently set big goals and met most of them to get to where they wanted to go. Why should you be any different? When you set goals, something inside you should say, "Let's get going. What am I waiting for?"

Leaders always think big when they set their goals. In order for a goal to be effective, they need one that's big enough to create excitement within them and among the team, one that will make everyone want to meet it. There's no excitement in just keeping up with someone. The excitement comes from being the best.

In the sports world, athletes consistently perform better against tough competition. Olympic swimmer Michael Phelps' journey to Beijing to win a record of eight gold metals attest to the goal-setting power of a great athlete. The same is true in business. If your goals are challenging and tough, they will bring out the best in you. Here is how each type approaches goals:

Type Ones. They are driven to achieve aggressive goals. They are sometimes prone to setting goals that are extremely difficult or impossible to reach. If you're Type One, although you may be very adept at determining what tasks need to completed to meet an established goal, you would be well advised to conduct a "reality check" to make sure you have both the time and resources to pursue the goals you set.

Type Twos. They are so deliberate when they enter into the goal-setting process that they can spend more time evaluating the "worthiness" of a given goal than it would take to complete the goal itself. If you're a Type Two, you must be decisive when it comes to setting goals. Once you set a goal you believe in, you can usually achieve it.

Type Threes. They like to set goals that are popular with others. As a result, they sometimes pursue goals that mean more to someone else than to them. If you're a Type Three you may encounter some difficulty maintaining your personal motivation to reach your goals. You would be well advised to focus your attention on selecting and pursuing goals that are important to you rather than someone else.

Type Fours. They will only set goals that they want to pursue as opposed to those that they need to pursue. For example, they would rather set a goal to win an essay contest and the subsequent award of a free trip to Hawaii than setting a goal to improve upon their communication skills by attending a course at the local community college. If you are a Type Four, you must recognize that your outlook on life can often be shortsighted. Unless you correct this problem, you may have difficulty moving up the leadership ladder.

Defining Your Goals

The goals you set for yourself must be specific, which means they must be clearly defined (i.e., twenty-five words or less) and have a start and completion date assigned to them. If they are made up of generalities, you will never know if you complete one. Your goals should be built on your strengths, not on your weaknesses. By calling on your strengths, you will be in a better position to pursue your goals with confidence.

Every goal you select should flow from your own motivations. There may be times when someone else's idea of what you should be doing may not match with your own. You will be required to work on a goal that your boss gives you even though it is not a goal that you want. How can you motivate yourself to meet your boss's goal? Make it a personal goal. Align it with your objectives. Sometimes you need to say to yourself, "My boss wants me to accomplish this goal. And if I do that, I'll look good in her eyes." That may be motivation enough for you. The more personal a goal is to you, the more commitment you'll give it.

Perhaps the greatest mistake people make when they define their goals is that they fail to also define the activities they will have to commit to in order to reach those goals. You must evaluate your plan as it fits into the structure of your work. Do you have the time and resources that you'll need to complete each defined goal that you have set for yourself? Here are the typical ways each of the personality types set their goals:

Type Ones. Exacting is a word that is often used to describe how Type Ones define any goal they set. As a Type One, you'll clearly describe your goals complete with start and completion dates assigned to each supporting task.

Type Twos. They are careful not to be too specific when they define their goals. As a Type Two, you want to assure yourself that you have flexibility to change the meaning and purpose of any goal you elect to pursue.

Type Threes. They do not appreciate the productive orientation that is implied by specific goal definitions. As a Type Three, you'll establish specific objectives for your goals but will only share that information with a few trusted associates.

Type Fours. They are often afraid to admit that they are even pursuing specific goals to anyone. As a Type Four, in your mind goals demand a serious amount of attention and work to complete. You don't like to be tied down to any specifically defined work-related goals.

What steps can you take to overcome the challenges your personality type has in setting clear, achievable goals?

Mixing Your Goals

Mix your short-range goals with your long-range goals. Short-range goals are the ones you'll complete in less than three months; long-range goals will take longer. Pursue short-range goals to keep your enthusiasm and motivation in high gear. Nothing is more invigorating than being able to tell yourself, "Well, I finally did it. I met a tough short-range goal, and it feels good." To balance things out, complement your short-range goals with long-range goals. One of the advantages of setting long-range goals is that they can neutralize the frustrations you may encounter while pursuing short-range goals. For example, your long-range goal may be to become the vice president of your organization. Suppose you set a short-term goal to pass the CPA exam to help you get there, and you fail the first exam. Yes, you are frustrated, but in the perspective of your long-range goal, it's only a temporary setback. You have time to figure out what you did wrong and take the exam again. Here are the ways in which each of the personality types mixes short-term and long-term goals:

Type Ones. They are well adapted at setting both short-range and long-range goals with ease. Their goal-driven personality thrives on the challenge of achieving what they set out to accomplish. If you're a Type One, you will rely on short-range goals as an incentive to reach more difficult long-range goals.

Type Twos. Being the creative thinkers that they are, Type Twos tend to set short-term goals that supplement their long-term goals. The end result is that their long-term goal is, in reality, a combination of several short-term goals. As a Type Two, you would be well advised to concentrate on setting goals that are distinct from each other.

Type Threes. They are better at setting short-term goals over long-term goals. The achievement of meeting their short-term goal objectives offers them an opportunity to display their progress to their peers. However, if you're a Type Three leader and you want people to follow you, you need a believable vision that contains both long-term and short-term goals.

Type Fours. They will support whatever goal is popular with little regard as to whether it's a short-term or long-term goal. This can cause problems if they find themselves committed to supporting a long-term goal that will require a significant effort on their part, after the celebratory party is over. If you're a Type Four leader, you need to address the different level of commitment required to endorse a more complex long-term goal before you commit to it.

Working on Your Goals

Goals are made up of tasks. When you successfully complete all of the tasks in a goal, you've met your goal. If you don't have a plan in place to work on your goals daily, you qualify as a goal-dreamer. These are the people who set goals but who have no plans or intentions of working their goals. They'll tell you, "Someday I'm going to be financially independent. I've got a great plan, but I haven't had time to work it yet." Charlie Cullen, the late leadership advocate, expressed the need to consistently work on goals when he said, "The opportunity for success does not come cascading down like a torrential rain fall, but rather it comes slowly, one drop at a time. Work your goals every day and they will become a reality." Here are some ways each of the personality types work their goals:

Type Ones. They are action-oriented individuals, almost to a fault. They are so task oriented that they will often get up before sunrise and methodically write down specific tasks they plan to complete that day. Before the day is over, they often will have "checked off" the tasks they completed. If you're a Type One, you can become aggravated over what you did not complete on your checklist. If you find this happening to you, try maintaining a weekly, rather than a daily checklist.

Type Twos. Analytical Type Twos will often spend a disproportionate amount of time determining when specific tasks need to be started and when they need to be completed. As a result, you will often find them "re-doing" their task list because something did or did not happen according to schedule. If you're a Type Two, you'd be better off focusing your attention on the major tasks rather than the minor tasks.

Type Threes. They are not generally task-driven individuals. Although most will have created a list of tasks that must be completed to achieve a goal they're pursuing, their task start and completion dates will be, at best, vague. Easygoing is their motto. As a Type Three, you should concentrate on the scheduling mechanics of task start and completion dates.

Type Fours. "Whenever" is the word that Type Fours will often use when they are asked when they'll complete specific goal-oriented tasks. They don't like committing to completion dates to anybody, including themselves. If you're a Type Four, you need to become more aware of the fact that meeting a commitment is an integral part of a leader's character.

Owning Your Goals

Every goal you set must be yours, even if they are given to you by someone else. You own them! If you have set a goal only because you are trying to please someone else, it's not really a goal; it's an assignment. Your goals should help you do the best you can each day while preparing you for a better tomorrow. After all, the future is where you're going to spend the rest of your life. Here is how each of the personality types deals with goal ownership:

Type Ones. They will quickly let their bosses know what goals belong to them and which belong to someone else.

Their power-oriented personality thrives on the achievement of reaching goals that have specific meanings to them.

Type Twos. They are perfectionists who will sometimes elaborate on exactly who owns any part of goals that they are pursuing. They may break each goal down into an exact percentage by ownership: I own 35 percent of this goal, my coworker owns 65 percent, etc.

Type Threes. They are indecisive when they address the issue of who owns the goals they're pursuing. They are uncomfortable admitting that they own 100 percent of a goal, but they also have a difficult time determining who owns specific parts of any one goal.

Type Fours. Self-oriented Type Fours will quickly select the parts of a goal that they like and will allocate the parts that they don't like to anyone they can find.

SETTING GOALS FOR YOUR EMPLOYEES

By now you should have a clear idea of how to set and accomplish goals and what your own strengths and limitations are regarding goals. Now apply these same lessons and methods to your employees, using both the power of your personality and your understanding of the personality types that make up your team.

What does it take to keep your employees motivated? The key is to encourage them to focus on the goal-oriented priorities of your organization. The ongoing successful completion of goals will drive their motivation. Without the attainment of goals, the team lacks motivation. Follow the same steps, outlined above, in setting your team's goals that you followed in setting your own:

1. Define team goals.
2. Mix long- and short-term team goals.
3. Work the team goals.
4. Help the team to own its goals.

Unfortunately, on many teams, employees seem to lack concentration. They may know what they should be working on but somehow, they never seem to accomplish those objectives. If this is the case with your team, you must ask some basic questions:

- What is the current level of motivation among your team members?
- Do they know what your organization's mission is and what its goals are?
- Do the team members know what goals have been assigned to them?
- Is their level of motivation stagnant?

If you want to see how you're doing motivating your employees to work on their goals, measure it. Ask yourself, "On a scale of one to ten (ten being high), how would I rate the overall level of motivation in my organization now?" Yes, this is a subjective measurement, but it should give you an indication of how motivated your people are. Then ask your employees the same question: "On a scale of one to ten, how motivated are you to help meet the goals of our organization?" Also ask them, "Do you know what the goals are for the organization?" Compare their answers to your answer.

As I indicated above, goals affect the motivational drive in each of the personality types differently. Here are some suggestions for how to approach goal-related problems with each of your four types of employees:

Type Ones

Type One employees are usually ready to aggressively pursue every goal you've set for them. They are committed to goals and objectives. However, because of their tenacious nature, they will often overcommit to more goals than it's possible to complete. They demand actions and results from themselves as much as they do from others and can become frustrated when they abruptly realize they are not successfully completing their goals.

If this applies to any of your Type One employees, reduce the number of goals that you have set for them to a manageable number. For example, let's assume the employee has taken on ten goals to accomplish over the next twelve months. You believe that she only has time to complete five of these goals. Select the goals that are most important to you, and put the others on hold. When she completes one of the goals on her list, replace it with an "on hold" goal to keep her active inventory of goals to five. Every now and then, remind the employee that her life won't end if she doesn't reach all of the goals on her list during the year.

Type Twos

Type Two employees are highly disciplined and have goal-oriented personalities. They're also perfectionists and as a result are critical of themselves. They are always "almost ready" to get started on their goals, but they worry about whether or not they can complete all of the goals they have set for themselves. They also tend to set unrealistic goals that they can't complete. Over time, if insecurity sets in they will challenge their own capabilities. This is unfortunate because most Type Twos are blessed with creative talents, which they often hide because of the insecurities that are associated with not completing their goals.

If you have a Type Two employee in this situation, ask him to sit down in a quiet location and list the uncompleted goals that he has set for himself over the past six months. Have him record the start and completion date that he established and in ten words or less, identify why he has not completed each goal. When he shows you his evaluation, offer him your evaluation.

- Were his goals realistic and obtainable?
- Were his completion dates realistic, taking into account his workload?
- Did he clearly establish the criteria for determining when each goal would be successfully completed?

The answers to these questions should help your Type Two employee better understand the goal-setting process.

Type Threes

Type Three employees have a tendency to select low-risk goals that they know they can accomplish. When it comes to goal setting, they tend to be uncommitted and are often unwilling to set goals because they want to always feel secure. The potential failure of not completing a goal may cause their feelings of insecurity. Type Threes do not want to introduce any more risks into their lives than they have to.

If you have a Type Three employee, you must establish a list of goals that are meaningful and important to her. Solicit suggestions from her. Go over with her what issues are important, and ask her to suggest goals that will help not only the business but will also help her accomplish what she wants out of life. Suggest that she read any material that emphasizes the importance of goals. When you believe she has honestly convinced herself about the value of the goal-setting process, proceed to the next step: Get her to start working on goals. This is where you'll find out if the employee is capable of living up to your expectations.

Pick one goal—not the easiest or most difficult one—that you have assigned to each of your Type Three employees, a goal that fits in the middle of the difficulty scale. Ignore all of the other goals and get them to work on accomplishing it. When each employee successfully completes that one goal, announce their success to your staff and celebrate. After the celebration, pick at least two goals and start the process all over again.

Type Fours

Type Four employees are always looking for a pen and pad of paper to write their goals on, but they can't find a pen. They tend to be disorganized and would rather focus on more immediate issues like planning for their vacation or puttering with minor concerns than to waste time developing long-term strategic goals. It's difficult for them to commit to anything that takes priority over their desire to always have a good time.

If you have a Type Four employee who is uncomfortable about setting goals, then encourage him to visit the library. Ask him to check out books that address the basics of how to set goals. He needs to learn all that he can about the importance of goals, how they're set and completed in a timely manner. When the employee has a solid understanding of the goal development process, sit down with him and mutually establish a set of goals that he can work on. Ask him two questions:

1. Do you understand what you must do to commit to and complete a goal that you set for yourself?
2. Do you understand how the goals make it possible to achieve what's important to the organization?

If his answer to either question is "No," send him back to the library to check out more books on the importance of setting goals in life! Spend time telling him about a few goals you've met and how they helped the company. (i.e., "I once had a goal to reduce our overseas shipping costs. I contacted four vendors, got price quotes ... etc. In the end, I saved the company $100,000! We used that money to finance a new position in the manufacturing department.") If the employee answers "Yes" to both questions, with his participation, set completion dates for goals that you have established for him. Closely monitor his progress.

All goals—both yours and your employees—must be realistic. If you or your team members set goals that are unrealistic and, as a result, consistently miss them, you could seriously impact your ability to motivate yourself and your team. A high failure rate could even affect the degree that you're willing to set new goals. Although you are encouraged to set challenging goals, make sure they're reachable.

PUTTING IT ALL TOGETHER

Before you establish your goals, focus on what it is you want to accomplish in your life. Break your wish list down into short-term (less than a year) and long-term (more than a year) objectives. Does each objective fit in with where you want to go as a leader? Are they realistic goals? When you have developed your list, begin laying out the steps and time that are needed to complete each goal. Write out each goal, specifying what you need to do to complete it, when you'll do it, and what you will have accomplished (i.e., something that is important to you) when it's completed. Ask your employees to go through the same exercise for the goals that you have helped them establish.

By doing this for yourself and your employees, you'll have taken an important step in moving from someone who manages employees to someone who can lead them.

Relationship Attributes of the Personality Types

TYPE ONE	They like to develop relationships with people who have assertive personalities, are goal oriented, and are highly ambitious.
TYPE TWO	They like relationships with detail oriented people who are analytical and creative in everything they do.
TYPE THREE	They will seek relationships with people that in their judgment are good people who can be trusted.
TYPE FOUR	They enjoy developing relationships with outgoing people who have socially oriented personalities.

CHAPTER 7

Building Powerful Relationships

The relationships you develop with team members as well as with your supervisors will become the cement that will hold together the leadership position you're building.

TAKE YOURSELF OUT of your work environment for a moment and assume that you own a farm, which is the sole source of your livelihood. Consider how ridiculous it would be if you forgot to plant in the spring, played golf all summer long, and then tried to get all of the planting done in the fall, when it was too late. When farming, you have to follow a consistent, scheduled process if you want to reap the rewards of what you sow. No shortcuts are allowed—you must always keep the long-term goal of a bountiful harvest in mind.

This same principle applies to human relationships, particularly those that are work-related. In the short term, you might get by making favorable impressions using your charm and pretending to be interested in the well-being of your friends and associates. Eventually, your true motives will rise to the surface and your short-term relationship will disappear because you didn't take the time to understand their personalities, learn what turns them on and off, and how to inspire them. There are no shortcuts in relationships.

On the other hand, if you take the time to develop lasting relationships with long-term staying power, they'll be rock solid. This chapter builds on applying everything you've learned so far. We'll show you how to use inspirational techniques to get people who are a vital part of your personal life to help you achieve the goals and objectives that are important to you. We'll show you how to build strong relationships with your team members. You'll discover how long-term relationships can and will reward you beyond your wildest expectations.

TYPES OF RELATIONSHIPS

Your level of success as a leader will be a function of how well you work with and relate to all of the people in your life. Successful leaders resonate with a wide circle of people and have a knack for building rapport with them. They know how to build and sustain solid human relationships that enable them to get extraordinary things done. They know nothing important gets done alone. Therefore, they have networks in place they can call on when they need support.

Developing solid relationships with the right people is critical if you expect to move up the leadership ladder. Relationships are key to your success as a leader, not just because of what other people can do for you, but because of what you can learn when you're around the right people. Good relationships broaden your perception and refine your ability to communicate.

When you become conscious about developing solid relationships and begin selecting people who can help you, you may have to dump some of the excess baggage you've been carrying around in your current network of relationships. That may include people you have known for a long time, but who have stopped contributing to your personal and professional life. Maintaining relationships is a time-consuming process and quite frankly, you don't have time to nurture useless or even damaging relationships. There are three types of relationships for you to consider.

Sinking relationships

A sinking relationship is like dead weight that can drag you down, hold you back, or sink you altogether. It's a relationship with a person who has low self-esteem and who is often avoided by others like the plague. The fact that you are seen talking to him can even place a cloud over your head. Such people are sometimes like Chicken Little—they believe that the sky is about to fall in at any moment. Whenever you meet with them, they will tell you what's wrong with anybody, from the janitor on up to the CEO. They'll tell you the company's about to go out of business, the food in the cafeteria is rotten, electronic bugs have been planted in the bathrooms.

Under the right circumstances, anyone can fall into the kind of depression that drags down everyone around them. But the different personality types each manifest a bit differently in this role:

Type Ones. Extreme Type Ones can become very argumentative with anybody who disagrees with their opinion or position. As a result, they refuse to listen to other people's ideas. Get rid of these types of relationships as quickly as you can, or they will sink you.

Type Twos. Unforgiving Type Twos can also sink you if they become caught up in past negative situations. Such people dwell on events that have already happened and will use them to make unrealistic projections about what they believe will happen in the future. If they refuse to live in the present, they are of no use to you.

Type Threes. Unmotivated Type Threes can sink any relationships you might have with them. They often lack direction and desperately look for anyone they can cling to for support and direction. You don't have time to baby-sit these people.

Type Fours. Extreme Type Fours who are always telling anyone who will listen how good they are as their way of justifying their existence in an organization. In reality, they have a difficult time actually accomplishing much of anything that's important. Type Fours in this mode of operation offer minimum value to any relationship.

Floating relationships

As the name suggests, a floating relationship acts like a life raft. If you should fall into a swamp, the life raft will be there to save you. People who have this kind of relationship with you are the ones you trust and can meet with to vent your frustrations. In most floating relationships, you aren't looking for valuable advice to solve your problems. Often, a few kind words are all that you need, such as "Yeah, that's a rough one. I don't blame you for being irritated." Floating relationships provide you with an important escape valve for your emotions, emotions you don't want to demonstrate in front of someone who can adversely influence your drive to become a leader.

Each of the four personality types can, under different circumstances, offer you a floating relationship, each with somewhat different elements:

Type Ones. Recognition is an important attribute of a Type One's personality. Rely on them to reinforce your need for recognition when you need it. If you want to know you're appreciated, they are the ones who can do it.

Type Twos. Your Type Two associates know how to embellish you with all of the appreciation you need, whenever you need it. They place a high value on personal relationships with people they trust.

Type Threes. If it is respect or praise that you need, see your Type Three associates. You can call on them to tell you what you're doing right. Conversely, they will be reluctant to tell you what you're doing that they think is wrong.

Type Fours. Type Fours are the performers of the organization. Sometimes it feels good just to be around them. If you're feeling depressed, see your Type Four friend and get an instant shot of enthusiasm to get yourself back on track.

Power relationships

Power relationships, properly used, can provide you with the people who can help you accelerate up the leadership ladder. When two people develop a power relationship, they instantly surround themselves with a sphere of energy that allows them to tap into each other for ideas and inspiration. Meeting with such people can drive your aspirations to their highest level. Power relationships can be developed from your professional or personal contacts. Regardless of the source, they always generate such a strong exchange of information that their relationship with you becomes a conduit for your creativity and brings out the best in you.

Each of the four types can become the basis of a power relationship that can benefit you.

Type Ones. These people are well versed at playing power relationship roles with their associates. They like to develop such relationships with people who have assertive personalities, are goal oriented, and are ambitious. Type Ones will often team with other power players to solve challenges.

Type Twos. They like to develop power relationships with detail-oriented people who are analytical and creative in everything they do. They will think first, before they will exercise any power or influence they might have over others. Type Twos do not like to use their power to adversely influence someone.

Type Threes. They will seek power relationships with people who, in their judgment, can be trusted to not abuse their power over someone else. For this reason, Type Threes will take whatever amount of time they feel is necessary to get to know you before they will establish a permanent power relationship with you.

Type Fours. Such people enjoy developing relationships with outgoing people who have socially oriented personalities. For this reason, Type Fours do not like to develop lasting power relationships unless the person with whom they have the relationship is part of their social circle of trusted friends and associates.

Your relationships should include a healthy mix of the four personality types as long as they are all working with you. However, if some adverse event like a health issue affects a person who's in your relationship sphere, you may suddenly have a sinking relationship to contend with. Do you drop them just because they have fallen onto some bad times? Of course not. What kind of leader would you be if you dropped one of your supporters just because they encountered problems? Do whatever you can to assist your fallen comrade while you carry out your leadership responsibilities within the organization.

BUILDING RELATIONSHIPS

You succeed or fail at having an opportunity to develop a relationship with people by the impressions you create in your initial meeting with them. In today's fast-paced work environment, deals are won or lost, careers are made or destroyed, relationships are established or broken all in a matter of minutes, based upon the impressions you make. Your first impression is the most important.

Ronald Reagan once said that up to 50 percent of the impressions you convey when you meet someone have nothing to do with what you actually say. Your nonverbal appearance, facial expressions, movement, and the tone of your voice are all major influencing factors, followed by what you say. As well, the impression you make will depend on the personality type of the person you're meeting. Here are several examples of how to build first-impression relationships with the different personality types:

Type Ones. First impressions are formed in only a few minutes with Type Ones, because they have short attention spans. If you fail to make a good impression in this time frame, it becomes much more difficult, if not impossible to develop a solid relationship with them.

Type Twos. Twos are all about trust. If you fail to capture their trust in your first meeting, you will have to overcome the issue in follow-up meetings with them. Type Twos are impressed by people who know what they're talking about and can demonstrate that they have courage of their conviction.

Type Threes. As with Type Twos, the primary first-impression issue for a Type Three is trust. Carefully probe them with questions to identify what trust issues are important to them if you want to develop a lasting relationship with them.

Type Fours. They are not impressed by people who adhere to the "what they are supposed to look like and say" within the political confines of their organization. What you say and how you say it with sincere meaning and conviction is more important to Type Fours. If you need to establish a relationship with them, you will have to work for it because they are reluctant to form a relationship on initial encounters.

ESTABLISHING A NETWORK

A network is an organized collection of personal contacts you can rely on when you need help or information. Sometimes you may meet a person who doesn't appear to fit directly into your leadership plan, but your intuition tells you this person is worth knowing. That may be reason enough to build the relationship with him. You do that not by asking yourself, "What can he do for me today?" but rather "What might he be able to do for me in the future?" The proper network technique is the reverse question: "What can I do for this person today?" If you consistently put people ahead of what you want from them, you'll develop powerful personal relationships in your network.

When you start building a network, include as many people as you can. That's okay because it doesn't hurt to practice your communication hooks covered previously. However, networking is a contact sport and you'll quickly discover that it's time-consuming to keep in contact with a lot of people. As a rule of thumb, if you can't contact everybody in your immediate network at least once a month, your network is too large. You will not be able to take care of the relationships that you have established.

As your network grows, become choosier about who you'll allow into your network. An ideal network will include people who can help you expand your center of influence. They know exactly what they can do to help you when the need arises. For example, if someone in your network knows the executive director of a professional association and knows you want to make a presentation at the group's annual meeting, that person will call you. She will tell you the director is expecting your call because she has "greased the skids" for the presentation you want to make. That's how good networks function.

Inner-Circle Networks

An inner circle is the core team of your leadership network. It's made up of about ten people you can always count on. Your team members can include friends, family members, and associates in your professional world who all fit within the scope of what you want to accomplish as a leader. You've selected them because they bring out the best in you, and they want you to succeed. They also know that they can rely on you to help them succeed. There's no competitive threat; they will never talk behind your back, and they will always have your best interests at heart. If all this sounds great, then you're probably wondering why I suggest restricting your inner circle network to just a few people (i.e., ten). That's because your best personal relationships deserve two or more contacts a month, so ten may be all you have time for. Whatever number you pick to be in your inner circle, make sure you can maintain a solid relationship with them.

You should also maintain strong relationships with other people who can back up your inner-circle relationships. Backup relationships transmit good stuff about you every day through their own networks. They also act as receivers collecting valuable information from a variety of sources that they pass on to you. This group can be larger than your inner circle as long as you can maintain regular monthly contacts with its members. On occasion, you may need one of your alternates to replace an inner-circle member who, for example, retires and moves to Australia (though in this age of instant communication, that's not nearly the problem it used to be).

Use Your Time Wisely

Ben Franklin once said, "If you waste minutes, you will lose hours." I don't need to remind you that every minute or hour you waste can never be replaced. Think about the minute. It's nothing, right? There are 1,440 minutes in a day. So what if you throw a couple of them away. How many times have you heard your friends and associates say, "If I only had more time, I could have done it." Were you one of them?

The next time you schedule a meeting with an important candidate whom you want to include in your network but who has a busy schedule, see if he tells you, "You've got a couple of hours to make your point." His more likely comment will be, "Take ten minutes to convince me that your ideas are worth pursuing." Networks are time-consuming entities to build and maintain; so as you search for people to join your networking, use your time wisely. It will pay you big dividends throughout your career. Let's look at several ways you can improve your use of time:

Plan your day wisely. Do you assign the same priority to everything you do during the course of a day? If you do, then you'll severely limit the time you have to develop meaningful relationships. Leaders know how to identify their priorities on a daily basis, beginning each day so that they can leverage their use of networking time.

Don't let your time get stolen. Let's suppose you are in your office working on a critical project. Just when you think you have the solution to a major technical problem that has been plaguing the project from its conception, your phone rings. Reluctantly, you answer only to be reminded of your luncheon date with a "non-network" person, who proceeds to tell you about her nephew's wedding on Saturday and a bunch of other stuff you don't care about. You've just been robbed of twenty minutes of valuable project time plus whatever additional time it takes to recover your problem-solving frame of mind. If you're working on something important, never allow anybody to disrupt you and steal your critical time unless she or he is a crucial member of your network. Turn off your phone, turn off your e-mail, and turn off your cell and BlackBerry.

Avoid urgent requests. Most of them aren't urgent anyway. We often allow urgent requests, those events that apparently demand our immediate attention, to disrupt the time we have allocated to work our priorities. Urgent requests for your immediate attention typically come from a ringing phone. "Sam just turned in his resignation and if you don't talk to him before he leaves the building, he's gone." Assuming that Sam is not part of your network, you would probably be better off allowing him to leave the building to "cool off" before you talk to him anyway. With the exception of real emergencies, most urgent requests do not require your immediate attention.

Watch out for procrastinators. They're the ultimate time wasters, who put off everything that's important until the last minute. They'll come to you with an urgent request to help them out. Don't do it. They don't recognize the importance of your time, and they don't know how to manage their own time. Procrastinators have no place in your network. If you cave into their request, you will jeopardize the time you need to devote toward getting your own work done and building your network.

AVOID PESSIMISTS

Pessimists are negative about everything including themselves and believe in Murphy's Law: "Whatever is right will go wrong, and whatever is wrong will never be right!" They have no inhibitions about letting others know how they feel and use the big "no" word every chance they get. "I've tried it and it won't work" is one of their classic responses.

Pessimists are experts at destroying optimists. They are not conducive to your network goals, so avoid dealing with them as much as is possible. However, there may be circumstances in which you are will be forced to work with a negative person. Maybe he's your boss, a peer whom you need support from, or a subordinate you can't afford to lose. Your challenge when dealing with a pessimist is to get him to move from a fault-finding attitude to a problem-solving attitude. How do you do that?

I remember when I was struggling to get through high school algebra and the instructor told the class that if you multiplied two negative numbers together, you ended up with a positive number. I never understood why, but I accepted what she told me. Forty years later, I finally figured out what she was talking about. If a pessimist makes a negative statement and you counter with a positive statement, the pessimist becomes more negative in his beliefs. If, on the other hand, you counter his negative response with your own negative response, you can align yourself with him and open the door to a solution. For example, you might say, "I agree with your adverse position, Joan, based on my similar negative experience with her. She has been complaining about the lack of attention she's getting on her marketing project. Let's meet with her, assure her that she is doing a great job, and discuss what we can do to solve the problem." When two negative answers are combined, you can end up with a positive answer.

Pessimists can actually become an invaluable resource within your network if you learn how to use their skill sets. For example, suppose you have a great idea but you want to identify all of the problems you'll have to overcome to implement it. Present your idea to a pessimist. She will be quick to tell you everything that can go wrong with your idea. Listen carefully to what she has to say. You can discount any problems she presents that in your opinion are not relevant, but chances are she'll identify problems you hadn't thought of.

Always Be Positive

Although you won't find the word "positiveness" in the dictionary, it best describes a critical element that you will need to establish a top-notch network. Always be positive. A positive attitude rubs off on anyone you touch. Because you are predominately a positive person, people who meet and talk to you feel good about you. You will build better relationships, which over time become fulfilling. and long-term. Zig Ziglar, a nationally known development speaker, summed it up when he said, "Your success as a leader is directly proportional to the number of people you make happy and successful." Ziglar identified several ways to accomplish this:

Respect. Mutual respect is the foundation upon which any relationship must be built. If it doesn't exist on both sides of the relationship fence, there is no relationship. Trust, integrity, and confidentiality all help build respect.

Needs. You can get so wrapped up in your own daily routines that you ignore or fail to see the needs of others. When you respond to the needs of others you build relationships.

Security. A fulfilled relationship is covered with a security blanket. A strong relationship is one in which you can confide your deepest secrets to the other person and feel sure they will be safe. You've got someone with whom you can share your private thoughts, feelings, and needs in a secure environment.

Admiration. All of us have an innate desire to be admired by others. Mutual admiration is the cement that holds relationships together.

Communication. One of the biggest roadblocks to building strong relationships is the inability to communicate effectively. Understand what the other person is saying either verbally or in his body language and you're well on your way to developing a positive relationship.

Resolutions. Conflicts will arise in any relationship. You have a choice of either resolving the conflict or dissolving the relationship. You'll invest a significant amount of your time to build a lasting relationship. You can lose it in a second to an unresolved conflict.

Criticism. If you're perfect, you don't need criticism. For the rest of us, criticism is the stuff we rely on to improve ourselves. When someone asks you, "What do you think?" Assume they really want to know. Honest opinions must be in place for a lasting relationship to work.

Display your positive attitude by always saying something nice to everyone you meet. Sincere flattery can go a long way to paving the road to your success. We all know how good it feels when others say something nice about us. Take the initiative and share that same feeling with everyone you meet. Phrases like, "You have a nice office," or "That's a great tie you're wearing," will often do it. If you don't know what to say, just say, "It's great to see you." You'll be amazed at how much more responsive people will be when you first say something nice, even if you are meeting under adverse conditions.

GET CONNECTED

Unfortunately, you can't build an effective network if you're not culturally connected. I recently had lunch with a remarkable executive in his early forties with a Harvard MBA. Steve knows how to make the right decision almost every time. When I had lunch with him, he was a candidate for the CEO position at a well-respected Fortune 100 company. Although the current CEO told him he was a serious contender for the position, he wasn't. I knew it, Steve knew it, and the CEO knew it. Why? Because he wasn't connected.

When Steve joined the company five years ago, he focused all of his energies on getting promoted to CEO. He took over a struggling division and was told he had a year to make it profitable or it would be shut down. He increased sales fourfold and profits tenfold. His performance was so superior when compared to peers running other divisions that the company leader included Steve on his list of possible successors. However, Steve now realizes he won't get the job because his style doesn't fit into the corporation's culture. He deliberately chose not to join the culture, and it cost him the promotion. Corporate leadership culture is how the organization believes you should look, and perform to fit into the company's leadership role. Steve wore sports coats to work while his peers wouldn't be caught dead in anything other than three-piece suits. He was noisy. They were quiet. He was an independent entrepreneur who made decisions on his own. They were hierarchically oriented executives who checked with their bosses before making any key decisions. The bottom line is that if you don't fit into your organization's culture, you won't have an opportunity to develop the kind of relationships you're going to need to become one of their leaders. You have two choices: determine if you can adjust your personal style to fit into your organization's culture or find another organization that is more suited to your culture.

PUTTING IT ALL TOGETHER

The ability to work with people to develop relationships is an indispensable requirement to build an effective leadership network. A leader understands how people feel and he recognizes the thinking attributes of coworkers' and employees' personality types. A leader intuitively knows when some people like to feel special, so he's there to compliment them. If they need direction, he shows them the way. If their emotions are getting them down, he inspires them with new hope.

Adapt your own leadership style to the people who are in your life to develop meaningful and lasting relationships. You cannot be a truly effective leader, the kind people want to follow, unless you have relationships that you can count on. Nothing can be accomplished until you begin building a network as the foundation for building meaningful relationships. This can become a serious problem with many people who put off building a network until later, when they never seem to have enough time. Networks take time to develop so don't let this happen to you.

Motivational Attributes of the Personality Types

TYPE ONE	They are autonomous individuals who are self-determined to motivate themselves to accomplish whatever is important to them.
TYPE TWO	They rely on motivation to drive them to achieve constructive outcomes in their lives and the lives of the people they care about.
TYPE THREE	They view motivation as a catalyst that will help them to accomplish their personal goals and assure themselves of a positive future.
TYPE FOUR	They will use motivation to pursue goals that are important to them as long they don't require a major commitment on their part.

CHAPTER 8

Motivating Your Organization

Motivation is the fuel that successful and dynamic organizations run on.

WE HAVE EXAMINED how to develop the motivational aspects of your own personality. Now we'll put that power to work motivating your employees. We'll look at the personality types of employees and see how you can motivate each one.

Walt Disney believed that visions are what makes human motivation possible. Any person who could create the first sound cartoon, the first all-color cartoon, and the first animated full-length motion picture was definitely someone who had a high level of motivation and vision. But Disney's greatest masterpiece was created later in life: Disneyland. In his mind, he had a vision of an amusement park where the fantasy didn't just evaporate at the end of the movie. He wanted to create a carnival atmosphere where children and adults alike could see their dreams appear.

The power of motivation is an amazing thing. In addition to self-awareness, imagination, and vision, motivation is the single most important ability required to achieve and sustain high levels of productivity. Walt Disney relied on thousands of highly motivated people in his organization to help him build his life-long dreams. He knew that when people feel good about what they're doing, they will work their hearts out to accomplish anything you put in front of them. When you feel good, it's easier for you to understand information and make wise decisions in complex situations. That in turn helps you feel more optimistic about your ability to achieve goals, which in turn enhances your creativity. Now we need to see how to give others that same feeling and encourage them to reach their goals.

The ability to motivate not only yourself but everybody you rely on is at the heart of the leadership process. Why? Motivation is the spark that lights the fire within everyone who follows you. To help you light that fire, know the personalities of your team players. Each personality type responds to motivation in different ways. Type Ones search for ways to keep themselves motivated. Type Twos constantly evaluate their motivational drive to see if it's working. Type Threes tend to hide what it is that they want to accomplish to avoid any criticism. Type Fours are concerned about getting too motivated if it will lead to excess work.

MOTIVATION ASSESSMENT QUIZ

A leader who can help members of her organization acquire an enthusiastic and cooperative mood guarantees the success of that organization. As you move down the leadership road to success, recognize that different motivational techniques must be used on the different personality types in your organization to effectively achieve your goals. When you can consistently motivate everybody in your organization, your value to the organization as a leader will increase significantly. First determine the current motivational level of your team by answering these questions:

MOTIVATION WITHIN YOUR ORGANIZATION ASSESSMENT QUIZ

Rank how each of the following questions apply to your organization.	OFTEN (3 points)	SOMETIMES (2 points)	SELDOM (1 point)
Do people blame others for what goes wrong in your organization rather than themselves?			
Do you feel that the employees in general do not accept responsibility for what they do?			
Are employees often failing to take the initiative to report their activities and progress on key projects?			
If someone "drops the ball" on an important issue, will someone usually pick it up without direction?			
Are employees waiting to see if things will get better when serious problems already exist?			
Do you hear people saying a situation is out of control and there is nothing they can do about it?			
Do you observe people "covering their backsides" when things go wrong?			
Do most employees know what is expected of them on assignments that are given to them?			
Do you hear people saying, "It's not my job" and complain about why it is not getting done?			
Do many employees display a low level of ownership and responsibility when problems arise?			
TOTALS			

Score your responses as follows: Often = 3; Sometimes = 2; Seldom = 1

What's your total score from the ten questions in the Assessment Quiz? Access your score using this table.

Motivational Score Within Your Organization

TOTAL SCORE	ASSESSMENT
21 to 30 points	You have some significant problems in your organization. Talk to your people where the major motivational problems exist.
11 to 20 points	Although your organization appears to be stable, focus on motivating your people to shift to a more positive attitude.
10 points	According to your answers, your organization is totally motivated. Under your leadership, the organization should continue to excel.

Recognizing problems with motivation is a first step in building an outstanding organization. All organizations have some motivational problems. A good leader knows you cannot fix a problem until you admit it exists.

LEADERSHIP ATTRIBUTES AND MOTIVATION

In Chapter 1, you were introduced to the three indispensable attributes (commitment, communication, and competence) that all leaders rely on to succeed. As a leader, how you apply these attributes to not only motivate yourself but your followers is an important component of your overall success. That's because motivation causes success and conversely, success causes motivation. As long as you are the master at motivating every member of your team to excel, you will accomplish whatever you set out to do, so let's get started.

Indispensable Leadership Motivators

CHARACTER	A leader can motivate every member of his team because the team members trust the integrity of his character.
COMMITMENT	A leader has a passion for doing what they say they will do now and in the future because they are motivated.
COMMUNICATION	A leader knows how to speak from the heart and verbally communicate her thoughts so that they motivate others.
COMPETENCE	A leader knows how to develop an active learning program that enhances his leadership capabilities and competence.

CHARACTER MOTIVATORS

How a leader deals with the circumstances of their life tells you a lot about their character and how they use it to achieve what they want out of life. Adversity is a crossroad that makes a person choose one of two paths to take. The right path is the one that's motivated by character with integrity. The wrong path is one that's motivated by easy-way-out character traits. Every time they choose integrity, they become stronger and more motivated, even if that choice brings negative consequences. Sit back for a moment and examine the condition of your character. Ask yourself whether your words and actions match up all the time? When you say you'll finish an assignment, are you always motivated to follow through? If you tell someone that you'll make it to an event that is important to them, are you there for it? Can people trust your handshake as they would a legal contract?

As you lead others in your personal life and at work, recognize that your character is your most important asset. A leader's rock solid character forms the foundation of their motivational drive. A leader's character must not only stay above the line between right and wrong, it also must stay well clear of the gray areas. Character by default becomes a prerequisite to motivating anyone. If you don't have character, nobody including your employees, coworkers, and superiors will listen to you, let alone become motivated by what you have to say. Let's review how your employees' different personality types apply character motivators to get ahead:

Type Ones. Type Ones have strict guidelines that they use when they judge someone's character. They appreciate people who have "task-driven" characters. That is, they know precisely what needs to be done and they are not afraid to jump in and get the job done. Their task-oriented personalities form the foundation of their motivational drive.

Type Twos. Type Twos are emotional individuals who are prone to feed their emotions off of crisis situations, real or perceived. They also have good analytical minds. If they are convinced that you are sincere and possess a high-integrity character like they have, you will go a long way toward earning their respect and motivating them.

Type Threes. The stubborn nature of Type Threes can make it a challenge for them to maintain integrity in their character. They rely on their diplomatic nature to dictate their character attributes. They will often choose compromises rather than what they truly believe in to appease the people in their life.

Type Fours. They appreciate people who exhibit lively, interactive characteristics. A good way to motivate Type Fours is to enable them to concentrate on what they like doing. If you can do this, you will make yourself indispensable to them.

Commitment Motivators
Many people make life unnecessarily difficult for themselves by dissipating their energy through fuming and fretting. Rather

than commit to do something about whatever it is that's bothering them, they waste their time and energy doing nothing. Committing neutralizes fuming and fretting. It's the first step to effectiveness. Your employees must commit to something before they will be motivated to accomplish it.

There are four steps you must take your team members through in developing their commitment.

1. Assist them in determining in detail the specific actions and steps to take to get to where they want to go.
2. Help them establish a time frame that tells them when to start and finish each step.
3. Agree on a measurement for each step so they will know when they have completed a task to your satisfaction.
4. Establish a clear goal so they will know when they have resolved the problem.

Each of the four personality types will react differently to these steps. Here's how each of them view commitment motivational steps.

Type Ones. Commitment to work personal goals and objectives are extremely important to Type Ones. Those who lack commitment feel more helpless and unmotivated than the other personality types. To restore their commitment to their personal and professional life, they must return to the goal-setting strengths that are inherent in their personality type. Review all their goals and, if appropriate, establish revised objectives and new estimated completion dates.

Type Twos. They can lose their commitment because of their innate fear of failure. After all, their logic runs, if you are not committed to anything, how can you ever fail? However, this goes against their better judgment. They have the analytical strength to determine precisely why they have become uncommitted. Leaders must patiently take them through the steps necessary to meet their goals and, where necessary, revise those goals, tasks, and completion dates.

Type Threes. If you explore why Type Threes have lost their commitment, you will probably discover that it was because they didn't want to expend the extra effort required to commit themselves to a given problem. When you're motivating a Type Three to a commitment, explain not only your priorities but why each priority is important to them.

Type Fours. It is a challenge for a Type Four to commit to anything that isn't easy or fun. If you are working with a Type Four, recognize this fact as one of the inherent weaknesses of his personality type. Your first challenge is to find something for him to commit to, something he can get excited about. Follow through with him until that commitment is realized and celebrate his accomplishment. Then, motivate him to make another commitment, one not necessarily as fun or exciting as the first. Step by step, you'll lead the Type Four personality to commit to projects for the good of the company rather than merely for his personal satisfaction.

Communication Motivators

Getting people to listen to your ideas can be frustrating. Your first challenge is to sell your employees on listening. Concentrate on what you're saying and how you're saying it—particularly through your body language—as they fight off inner thoughts and feelings that are competing for their attention. Show them how your idea fits not only into your and the company's plans, but also how it links to their own expectations and concerns. Be patient as you build your ideas one word at a time. As you read through this section, keep these simple communication points in mind:

- Listen before you speak.
- Ask before you tell.
- Remember what you see is only half the story.
- Choose a response that moves you toward a desired outcome.

People are often concerned that your ideas may require a commitment from them to implement. You can counter those concerns by making it clear that they too will gain from the idea. Tell them up front what they're going to gain by listening to you. That will push their motivation button. At the start of your presentation, summarize the most intriguing part of your whole idea in one or two sentences emphasizing its benefits. Remember that the first two minutes of your presentation are critical. That's when your audience will decide to listen further to what you have to say or stop listening because they're no longer interested.

No matter what your idea or topic is, you have the power to make it stimulating and motivating. If you're excited, they'll be excited. And if you can make the topic exciting to your listeners, you'll sell them on your idea and convince them to get behind it.

Naturally, the various personality types react differently to communication. Here's a breakdown:

Type Ones. When you're attempting to get Type Ones to listen to you, start with a bang. Make sure you have something to say that's worth listening to and that will interest them. Are your thoughts organized and easy to grasp? Do you make your main points up front so that they'll think, "Hey, this may be a good idea that's worth listening to." If you drag out whatever you're trying to say, you risk losing your listeners.

Type Twos. Express your idea in the first part of the presentation and immediately check out your Type Two listeners to see if they understand and agree with your points. Be patient if they make objections, and encourage them to ask questions by asking, "Do you have any questions?" If they're not asking any questions, they may not be listening to your pitch. If they make a point that you like, tell them you agree with what they said. If they make a point that you disagree with, ask probing questions to make sure you understand exactly what's bothering them before you recommend a solution.

Type Threes. Sometimes Type Threes will appear to be quietly listening to what you're saying. But such appearances can be deceptive. Type Threes are polite and always want to seem interested in what others have to say. Don't take their attention for granted. Slow down and encourage them to ask questions. Through dialogue with them, you can more accurately assess their level of agreement with your proposals.

Type Fours. One of the best ways to link a Type Four's thinking with yours is to compare his understanding with what you have already said. For example, you might say, "Jim, do you agree with me that we both should present this idea to the executive committee?" If Jim isn't giving you any feedback, change your question into a joint ownership question. "Jim, would you be willing to make a joint presentation with me to the executive committee?" To motivate a Type Four to make a commitment, communicate with questions.

Competence Motivators

In order to become motivated to pursue a common cause, people must believe that their leader is competent to guide them wherever they're headed. They must also believe that that they themselves have the competence to achieve what's expected of them. To assure them that they have the relevant experience is developed by having them actively participate in a situation or functional event to accumulate the knowledge derived from doing something. If they doubt their abilities, they are unlikely to join in the crusade. Competence refers to one's track record and ability to get things done. It can refer to an individual's core technology (i.e., training, education, expertise, etc.) to complete specific tasks. In more general terms, competence can refer to an individual's motivation and drive to complete a task, where they are willing to take the time to learn about something that they know little or nothing about.

Relevant experience is a dimension of competence that is different from technical experience. As a leader, you must elevate the confidence your people have in their own competence as well as in yours. Here's how the different personality types react to different competence motivators:

Type Ones. To a Type One, competence is doing something that they know will work. They are not afraid to take on a tough challenge to demonstrate their level of competence to others. They admire people who display high competence levels, whether they are precision craftsmen, world-class athletes, or successful business leaders. Type Ones are very confident in their own level of competence.

Type Twos. Responsible people show up at work when they're expected to. But a highly competent Type Two takes showing up another step further. He doesn't just show up in body alone. He is disciplined and comes to work ready to win every day, no matter how he feels, what kind of circumstances he faces, or how difficult he expects a situation to be because he is competent in what he's doing.

Type Threes. Pleasant and agreeable, Type Threes continually search for ways to keep learning, growing, and improving their competence. They like to inspire and motivate others to do the same thing. While some people depend on their relational skills alone to get along, Type Threes combine their relational skills with high competence to reach new levels of excellence and influence.

Type Fours. Charismatic and enthusiastic Type Fours value the attributes of competence, but are reluctant to go the extra mile to take their own competence to a higher level. For them, okay is good enough. They are not interested in hitting home runs unless it's for something that they really care about. Only then will they improve their competence to make it happen.

TEAM MOTIVATORS

The era of the pompous leader who sets policy, delegates everything, and sits back waving his hands waiting for something to happen are over. We're now living in an era of hands-on organizations where everybody from workers to the CEO are responsible for making good things happen in a team environment. If you are working for an organization that is not operating in a team environment, consider getting out now. They won't last long.

There are thousands of different ways to motivate your team, and we can't cover them all here. To start, here's one story that illustrates the importance of good motivation. During an interview with *Sports Illustrated*, Fran Tarkenton, one of the greatest quarterbacks in football history, recalled a play his coach called where Tarkenton had to block. Blocking quarterbacks are as rare as three-dollar bills. The Minnesota Vikings, Tarkenton's team, were losing to St. Louis, and Tarkenton knew he had to call a surprise play to save the game. Nothing would surprise the defense more than if the quarterback became a blocker. The play worked; Tarkenton took out a tackler, and his teammate scored the game-winning touchdown.

Bud Grant, the Viking coach, came into the locker room after the game. Tarkenton waited for his expected pat on the back. It never came. Grant praised everybody involved in the play except Tarkenton. The quarterback later confronted Grant in the privacy of his office and asked, "You saw my block, didn't you coach? How come you didn't say anything to me about it?" Grant replied, "You don't need it. Yeah, I saw the great block you made. Fran, you're always working 100 percent out there so I figured I didn't have to tell you." Fran replied with, "Well, if you want me to block again, you do it yourself!"

The moral of the story is: Don't ever take any of your winning team members for granted the way Bud Grant did with Fran Tarkenton. If you're a team leader, keep your team motivated by touching each of your players at least once a day with praise and words of encouragement. If someone on the team is slipping, jump in and say, "What can I do to help?" Let's review how to motivate the different personality types on your team:

Type Ones. They are task-driven individuals who like to beat whatever schedule you give them. If you've given them a team assignment that has a deadline attached to it, Type Ones will motivate the entire team to beat the schedule. Everybody who is directly or indirectly associated with the team project will be impressed by the efforts your Type One employees put into the activities of the team to assure its success.

Type Twos. They are perfectionists and will closely monitor the quality effort of the team. If you make them responsible for monitoring the team's quality control, you will reinforce their motivation to produce outstanding results. They will actively solicit the advice and support of their team members to develop quality control.

Type Threes. These are inventive individuals who have lots of good ideas that they want to share with their team members. If you do everything possible to encourage their innovation, they will be motivated to offer new ideas for your organization. Even if you don't have a budget for prize money, offering them personal recognition will get you lots of innovative ideas from your Type Three employees.

Type Fours. They are carefree individuals who take on a team assignment as "just something else to do." No matter what the assignment, you must make it stimulating and exciting to get their attention. If you can do that, you will motivate them to expend extra energy on their team effort. Conversely, if they are not interested in the objectives of the team; they will expend a minimum amount of effort on the assignment.

Meeting Motivators

Like the weather, everybody complains about meetings, but few know what to do about them. Despite the fact that meetings, unlike weather, are a human creation, we often feel as if we have no more control over a meeting than we do the weather. However, we tend to believe that two or more heads are better than one when key decisions need to be made.

One scene in the movie *Wall Street* crystallizes why meetings break down and how they can get back on track. A large corporate meeting with hundreds of people in attendance is taking place, and company executives are arguing with impatient shareholders about why profits are down. The meeting is dissolving into chaos. In a sensible world, these forces should work together to solve their mutual problem. Instead, each special-interest group wants results that will benefit them. They're pulling apart instead of together.

One of the corporate executives grabs the microphone and shouts, "Greed is good." That single phrase captures a common theme among all the various groups in the meeting. Instantly they gel into a single force behind their newfound "greed is good" leader. Rather than arguing pointlessly, they start to discuss alternate ways the organization can maximize profits.

The initial problem in this fictional Wall Street meeting is the fact that no central theme has been established from the start of the discussion. It takes a disproportionate amount of meeting time to arrive at a theme that everyone agrees upon. You can show your qualities as an outstanding leader instead of just a manager by conducting effective meetings. In these meetings, focus on the central theme and a series of related objectives.

Much of people's impatience with meetings stems from the time it takes them to produce real value. No wonder nobody wants to attend a meeting. How often do you ask meeting participants to bring prepared thoughts into a meeting? Do you tell attendees the exact purpose of the meeting before they assemble? If you routinely ignore these steps, most of your meetings will take twice as long as they should because nobody has been given an opportunity to prepare. You'll be lucky if anything gets accomplished. Get hard-nosed about what you want to accomplish at every meeting you sponsor. Let's review how the different personality types of your employees can be motivated by using different meeting tactics:

Type Ones. They are impatient individuals who can get frustrated if they are required to attend long, drawn-out meetings. They are motivated to attend meetings that are focused on accomplishing specific goals and objectives. They like to attend meetings that are called to address complex issues.

Type Twos. They are analytical individuals who will actively solicit advice from the people whose opinions they respect. They like to be asked to give their advice on just about anything. When you allow them to offer you advice during the meeting, you open up a motivational side of their personality that you can count on to support your team. Listen to what they have to say, even if you disagree with their comments.

Type Threes. They like to be free of pressure, and they can become very uncomfortable if they are involved in a conflict during the meeting. For this reason, when possible don't ask them to attend meetings that are called to resolve confrontational problems. Coach them on techniques that they can use to accept more high-pressure situations.

Type Fours. They are impulsive individuals who do not like to be involved in a meeting where decisions have to be made. Let them know that they must learn how to become decision-makers if they want to get ahead in your organization. Coach them on how to become more creative and logical thinkers who can make decisions quickly.

People Motivators

Are you pulled between the need to slow down and sense of urgency about the problems you face? Are you frustrated because no matter how hard you try, there is still a big gap between your aspirations and the reality you face? Are you avoiding personal problems, staying late at work rather than going home? Are you clinging to a work ethic that says if you're not overworking, you are not succeeding? Whatever your reasons may be, it is time to stop overwhelming yourself with work. If you keep up a fast pace, you won't have time to pay attention to motivating others. Working hard and not smart will not move you forward. If you're continually overworked, chances are you haven't had time to pay attention to the people who can help you.

The true measure of how well you're doing is the number of people you've motivated to give their best efforts. When you adopt this approach, you will be amazed at the positive results you'll get. You'll get invited to key strategy meetings because your superiors believe you have something to offer. They'll start calling you for advice and opinions on difficult subjects. You'll be wanted.

To be a successful leader, you must motivate the people working for you based not only on their work performance but on the way in which they approach personal relationships. This is key in team building—getting the right mix of people together. Let's review the different personality types.

Type Ones. They are strong-willed individuals and value relationships with people who can "get it right the first time." They are not motivated to work with people who do not meet their high standards. Caution them to be more patient with people. Show them how relationships that they develop with people who need their assistance can become an important asset to their career. In this way you can motivate them to be more patient and thus more productive in a team setting.

Type Twos. They are sensitive individuals who like to acknowledge people for what they have done. Any chance you get, give them praise for a job successfully accomplished. "What a great presentation, George!" "I like your idea. Can we discuss it further?" When you tell people what they want to hear, they will support you and the team.

Type Threes. They are social individuals who like to help people develop themselves. Let them know that when they do this they are performing an important function for the team and for the organization, which you appreciate. If they are confident they're performing an important people-related function, you will solidify their support for all the people in your organization.

Type Fours. They are charismatic individuals who like to establish people networks throughout an organization. You can call on them if you need advice on who you should contact to help you solve a particular problem. Compliment them on their ability to relate to their teammates who have a diverse set of views and ideas.

PUTTING IT ALL TOGETHER

The ability to motivate your direct reports in your organization is at the heart of leadership. It's indispensable because motivation shows where you want people to go and lights the fire within everyone who follows your lead. Motivation is one of the most powerful tools you can use to accomplish your tasks. Your challenge is to provide the catalysts that will excite people. It's to help them get through tough times as well as good times.

To help you light the motivational fire, it is important that you know the personalities of your team players because each personality type is motivated in different ways. The art of motivating others does not have to be complicated. Sometimes simply saying "thank you" and meaning it may be all that it takes. Celebrating both individual and team accomplishments is another way of enhancing motivation within an organization. Always remember: *Leadership is a relationship with people.* People are much more likely to complete initiatives if their leader motivates them.

Confrontational Attributes of the Personality Types

TYPE ONE	They can become openly angry if they are confronted with a situation that is an affront to their beliefs.
TYPE TWO	They will avoid open confrontations whenever possible and will plan appropriate revenge strategies against the people who confront them.
TYPE THREE	They will control their anger if they are confronted with an adverse situation and will methodically plot a "come back" strategy.
TYPE FOUR	They do not like confrontations of any type and will often refuse to acknowledge or address people who confront them.

CHAPTER 9

Controlling Confrontations

Confrontations can destroy your relationships and damage your career if you let them.

ANYONE CAN BECOME angry—that is easy. But to be angry at the right person, for the right reason, at the right time, and in the right way—that is not easy. Media mogul Rupert Murdoch has been both praised and criticized for the unorthodox business strategies he used to build his company, News Corp., into a profitable media giant. How did he do it? As a leader, Murdoch never let his management team waste its energy bogged down in meaningless confrontations. He chose which battles to fight and was willing to dig into the core problems that caused confrontations in the first place. He then moved aggressively to implement a solution for every problem he discovered.

This chapter is filled with various examples that show you how to minimize your exposure to confrontations. You'll learn how to control conflicts with the different personality types so that they'll have a minimal disruptive effect on your personal and professional goals. You'll also discover how to recognize confrontational situations so that you can eliminate them before they get started.

HOW CONFRONTATIONS START

Confrontations result when a disagreement, a controversy, or a personal clash occurs between two or more people. The word itself connotes something serious and for this reason should be avoided as much as possible. As everybody knows from experience, conflicts are unpleasant. They can be disruptive to relationships, are often counterproductive, and can be costly to your career. People rarely walk away from a conflict situation as absolute winners. Unfortunately, conflicts are an inevitable part of human relationships.

A confrontation often starts with words, "You did this . . ." or "You're the one who is responsible for . . ." will generally trigger a hot confrontation that can quickly escalate into a conflict. If someone approaches you with confrontational words, you can often diffuse the situation with words like, "I'm sorry you feel that way. Can we discuss it?" or "Although I respect your opinion, we need to review . . ." Many times, the person confronting you just wants you to listen to him. Often, a few minutes of listening can do wonders to diffuse a potential conflict situation. Even if you disagree with him, allow your employee get his feelings into the open where they can be addressed. This is one of the best ways to resolve a conflict.

On the other hand, as a leader sometimes you have to exercise your authority to turn off a confrontation. Despite its negative style, the command-and-control approach holds an important place in a leader's repertoire as long as it is used judiciously. The technique is particularly effective when time is of the essence. For example, if you are in an urgent turnaround situation, you may not have time for lengthy discussions with your reports about a particular course of action. In such situations, the commanding style can be very effective. As well, you can use it to eliminate useless business habits and shock people into accepting new ways of doing things. Sometimes it's also necessary when dealing with problem employees.

WHO ARE CONFRONTERS?

A confronter is a person who, for whatever reason, likes to cause confrontations between as many people as he can. If you say something is white, he'll argue with you that it's black. If, in desperation, you agree that it's black, he'll find a way to continue the confrontation. We have all faced people like this during our lives. Such employees are capable of using their aggressive behavior and all of the influence they can muster to destroy your leadership position.

If you are confronted by an aggressive person, what steps can you take to neutralize the situation? If you're right—and as a leader, you should have confidence in your own opinions—hold your ground and do not change your stated position. If you don't do this, your antagonist will perceive it as a sign of weakness. Like a vampire, he will move in for the kill. Avoid going on the defensive, but don't immediately respond by attacking. Restate your positions in clear terms. If she counters your position with another position, say nothing unless you are asked for an opinion. If the confronter asks what you think about her position, simply say, "You're certainly entitled to your opinion." It is very difficult for dedicated confronters to effectively respond when you step away from the confrontation.

Even if you believe the confronter's accusations are unfounded, leave the door open so that she has room to back off. She may be able to damage your career, so never close the door in her face if you can avoid it. If you can reach a peaceful settlement with a confronter, you win. If you are not used to playing the role of a diplomat or negotiator, get used to it when you're dealing with a confronter. Skillful diplomacy is a key element of leadership. Playing these positions allows you to move in and out of an argument without damaging your employee's ego. It gives her a chance to see what you're made of as she takes a measure of your character and commitment. Over time, if she discovers you are too hard a nut to crack, she'll move on to another potential victim and leave you alone.

As you might expect, each of the four personality types react to a confrontational situation in different ways. Some of this depends on the event that triggers the confrontation. For example, if your organization is going through rapid growth and there is a lot going on, action-oriented Type Ones—who don't mind confrontations—may come to the fore. They'll often be aggressive and actively seek out confrontations that you'll need to defuse.

In that same situation the fury of all the changes may bother Type Twos, who tend to get emotional and confrontational if things are moving faster than they would like. They're detailed-oriented individuals who like to analyze everything before it happens, which is impossible in a fast-moving work environment. To help them get acclimated to the changes that are occurring, provide them with as much detailed information as you can. In this way, you'll avoid confronting them and instead get them working with you.

Because they are unsure of themselves in the first place, an avalanche of changes can confuse the heck out of Type Threes. They won't know which way to go or what to do, and they may react by becoming confrontational. It's up to you to lead the way and tell them exactly what they must do.

Like their Type Three counterparts, Type Fours lack direction and tend to be disorganized under the best of circumstances. All of the change will also be confusing to them and cause them to become confrontational unless you explain clearly to them what's going on. Remember, they like to be followers, not leaders.

Here are several confrontational situations that you may encounter within your organization.

CONFRONTING THE NEARLY RETIRED

Yogi Berra once said, "The game isn't over until it's over, but eventually, it's over." For nearly retired employees, that day may come long before their final paycheck gets processed. As they reconcile themselves to the fact that they have risen as high as they are going to rise in the organization, regardless of what they do, they can become demoralized and angry. Creeping retirement can become a cancer that eats away at an individual's motivational well-being and causes him to move into a confrontational state of mind. The challenge of motivating near-retirees is to convince them that setting performance records should still be very important to them. Encourage them to hit the finish line at a pace that will leave their mark on the wall for the others to follow. Remind them that one of the best ways to end a career is by showing younger workers how far they have come so that others can follow in their footsteps.

The Situation

Good old Bill is driving you crazy. When you ask him to do something, he just looks up at you, smiles, and says he'll look into it. You tell him you don't want him to just look into it, you want him to do it—now. He keeps on smiling and gives you his standard speech that you've learned to hate: "Son, I've been here a long time. This company will continue on whether or not I do or do not do what you want me to do. Trust me when I say I'll look into it before I retire in six months." Unfortunately, Bill is the only person you have who's qualified to handle this assignment.

Type Ones. If Bill has a Type One personality, he was probably a real "power burner" in his day. You can rest assured that he knows how to play the confrontational game with the best of them and he's trying to manipulate you. If Bill has a lot of contacts from his years with the company, be careful. If you have a confrontation with him, he will probably discredit you with as many of his contacts as possible. Remember, he has nothing to lose since his career is almost over. Play along with Bill as best you can until he retires. Find someone else to do the assignment that you wanted Bill to do. You're going to have to train someone to take over his responsibilities anyway, so start now. This will help undermine Bill's ability to confront you as well as challenging him with the reality of his coming retirement.

Type Twos. If Bill has a Type Two personality, he is extremely loyal to the company. His seeming lack of enthusiasm for the assignment you are trying to give him is a cover job to get what he wants. He really wants to be appreciated and to know that he can still provide a valuable function to the company. Explain to Bill how important this assignment is to the company. When you tell him he's the best qualified to do the job well, stand back and watch Bill perform.

Type Threes. Even though Bill appears to be dancing around the assignment you've given him, the obedient nature of his Type Three personality provides you with a way to get him back on track. In a firm tone, tell Bill that you don't want him to look into the assignment—you want him to do it! Don't be afraid to tell him that if he can't give you the commitment you need, you'll find someone who can. If he chooses that approach, tell him that you will look into accelerating his retirement date since you don't need him anymore. Bill will rise to the challenge and do the job in record time.

Type Fours. People with Type Four personalities like to play games if they can get away with it. Bill thinks he's being clever when he tells you he'll look into your assignment. He also believes he can get away with it since he's about to retire. If you do not take control of the situation, Bill will continue to play his confrontational games. Ask Bill if he wants to be treated just like everyone else in your organization even though he plans to retire in six months. When he says yes, tell him that if he cannot commit to your assignment, you will write him up, just as you would any other employee. He will quickly stop playing his game and readily accept the assignment.

CONFRONTING DISHONESTY

As a leader, you must be willing to employ hardcore tactics to halt lying, cheating, and stealing, and maintain the integrity of your employees. To assure your credibility, be prepared to fire the first person who lies, cheats, or steals from the organization. Although you can't wipe out skullduggery altogether, you can take steps to cut it down to manageable size. To keep people on their best behavior, eliminate the conditions that encourage unethical acts in the first place. Add safeguards for activities such as cash transactions that could lead to unethical conduct. It's a lot easier to eliminate a tempting condition than it is to figure out who did it after the fact.

The Situation

When Kathy, the vice president of personnel walks into your office and asks if she can speak with you off the record, you wonder what she has on her mind. Taking the initiative, she abruptly shuts the door, takes a seat, and proceeds to tell you some things about your organization that you find appalling. "As you know, our CEO has asked my department to conduct an integrity audit on the company. Let me tell you what I found in your organization: Twenty people lied when they were asked if they were smokers or nonsmokers on the company's life insurance form. Sixty percent of the PDA computers that were issued to your staff over the last three months cannot be located. The assumption is that your people have taken them. I'm sorry that I have to be the one to dump the bad news on you, but better that you hear from me first, rather than the CEO."

You agree and thank Kathy for informing you of the dismal news first. You ask her to conduct another audit after you have had a chance to address the problem with your staff. She agrees, and as she leaves your office, you can't help but wonder if your organization is made up mostly of liars, cheats, and thieves.

How do you go about changing a dangerous set of habits within your organization? You plan to hold a series of town hall meetings with everyone in the organization to stamp out the problem before it stamps you out. Since all four personality types will be present in each meeting, you must present the issues in a way that will get the attention of each personality group.

Type Ones. To grab the attention of your Type One employees, at the start of your meeting show the dismal percentages that Kathy presented to you. Follow up the town hall meeting with individual sessions. Constantly brief your Type One employees about their ethical responsibilities. Remind them that you are not an undercover investigator, but rather a leader who is trying to prevent dishonesty within the organization.

Type Twos. Because of their analytical mindsets, your Type Two employees may question the accuracy of Kathy's statistics. Spend some of your presentation time showing them why you believe the numbers are statistically accurate. When you have their attention, tell them what actions you are taking to prevent this from happening again and inform them that the audits will continue until the problem is resolved. Remember that Type Twos have a high regard for organizational rules and regulations.

Type Threes. You'll lose the attention of your Type Three employees unless you address the commitment that you expect from them. In your initial presentation, mandate that the conduct in question must cease and desist. Back your order up with a warning stating that any employee caught lying, cheating, or stealing from the company will be immediately terminated. In follow-up meetings with Type Threes, talk to them about how important ethical issues are and how easy it is to overlook them.

Type Fours. As a leader, you are responsible for making sure that all of your subordinates are aware of the company's ethics policies. Periodically remind your Type Fours about the code because they will quickly forget it. If they forget the code, misinterpret it, or fail to realize how it applies to what they're doing, review it with them again. They may not take you seriously until you tell them that periodic audits will be conducted to determine who is violating company policy. Stress that such violations will be grounds for immediate termination.

CONFRONTING PRIMA DONNAS

Prima donnas are vain, undisciplined employees who find it difficult to work under direction or as part of a team. Almost every organization has them. Start-ups and growing companies actually need them—they are self-assured individuals who have all of the answers—or at least think they have. If properly motivated, they can be very productive, imaginative, and creative employees. But their huge thirst for acclaim and autonomy, while driving them to excel, can also spark confrontations, depress morale, and kill productivity in your organization. How do you drag your superstars back down to earth?

The Situation

Your salesman Bob is driven and phenomenally productive. The trouble is, Bob knows it, and he's been driving his coworkers nuts with confrontations and displays of poor behavior. Things have gotten so bad that several of your salespeople have complained to you about the problem and have threatened to quit if it continues. You're hearing that Bob is so confrontational that nobody's able to get their work done. What can you do to eliminate Bob's tendency to cause confrontations?

Type Ones. Prima donnas who are Type Ones can take several different forms, ranging from the raging egomaniacs to the more subtle passive-aggressive types. The one thing all Type One prima donnas possess is a tendency to put themselves ahead of their team members. Like a wild mustang, you have got to break them of that habit. Type Ones also don't shrink from confrontations, but you can be direct in dealing with the problem. Call Bob into your office and tell him point blank what you and the sales team think of him professionally. Include both the good and the bad, but stress the problems he's creating by his conduct. If he challenges your accusations, invite him to attend a meeting of his peers to hear what they have to say firsthand. Focus your remarks on the good of the organization and the possibilities for advancement if he mends his ways. If he rejects your suggestion, continues to disregard his coworkers, and argues his case, you may have to fire him.

Type Twos. Prima donna Type Twos want to know that their feelings are understood by everyone. If you attempt to burst their bubble and tell them that in spite of their excellent exploits, nobody is behind them, they may hand you their resignation. If Bob is a Type Two, handle this situation with kid gloves by patiently coaching him on how to cultivate a working relationship with people. Assure him that although his ideas are great, it does no harm to seek out other people's ideas to improve upon his own.

Type Threes. Type Threes can be very insecure individuals and it is not uncommon for them to use a prima donna front to hide their insecurities. You need to find out what is causing Bob to feel insecure before you can break him of his confrontational behavior. To get at the heart of the problem, be prepared to ask him a lot of questions. These can be both personal and professional: "Bob, is something bothering you? Can we talk about it? Maybe I can help?" If he tells you that people don't understand what he is trying to say, coach him on some communication techniques he can use to overcome this common problem.

Type Fours. Type Fours, with their self-centered personalities, are common prima donnas. One of the best ways to handle them is to confront them as soon as you are aware of the problem. Ask Bob candidly and in an unthreatening manner what is triggering his behavior. Often, the real problem behind Bob's behavior is something other than his swelled head. His feelings of insecurity could be causing him to boast about himself to cover his feelings. He needs to recognize his insecurity problem before you can help him overcome it. Hold several private sessions with him to help uncover the causes of his insecurities.

CONFRONTING CHANGE

In 1905, football was a low-scoring sport of running and kicking the ball. A bunch of guys in leather helmets would line up on the football field and see if they could keep the other team from making a three- or four-yard gain. A four-yard gain was a big deal. When the forward pass was legalized in 1906, it was suddenly possible to gain more yards with the flick of a wrist. During the first season, all but one of the teams stayed with their conventional running games. Recognizing that football had entered an era of change (i.e., the forward pass), the coaches at St. Louis University quickly adapted to a passing offensive game. That season, they outscored their opponents 402 to 11 because they were willing to change!

Each day, we face changes that are as challenging as the forward pass was to football. Every time we turn around, the rules of the game have changed. As a leader, you can no longer afford to recycle, modify, or revise the conventional wisdom of the past. The pace of the changes in the new millennium will make the past couple of decades look like a walk in the park.

Tim Nelson, a great surfer and friend of mine, once told me, "The time to change is when you don't have to, when you're on the crest of the wave, not when you're in the trough." Changes are events that can affect employees who are reluctant to change.

A big part of the problem is that many people see change as something they have no power over. When people are bothered by something they can't control, it can affect their work. Some may be distracted, while others will spend excessive time venting their feelings or working off their negative emotions through confrontations, all of which are counterproductive. The end result is always the same—productivity takes a nosedive and people lose their motivation to work.

The Situation

The executives in your organization are in the process of negotiating an acquisition. Some employees view this as a negative event, since they're worried about layoffs, changes in their benefits, or other consequences. The potential acquisition is causing ripples throughout the organization. You are disturbed by all of the "hall talk" that is taking place about the pending acquisition. To help neutralize the situation, you have decided to hold a series of one-on-one meetings with the members of your team. You'll need to approach each meeting by keeping in mind the personality type of the employee you're meeting with.

Type Ones. The potential threat of being laid off as a result of the acquisition is a direct assault to Type Ones who believe they are invincible. For them, the prospect of a layoff implies that they may have been wrong, which can have a devastating effect on their motivation.

To neutralize this situation, you need to explain to each Type One employee in very logical terms that the acquisition has nothing to do with him or her personally. Be honest with your Type One employees and if the acquisition will potentially offer them new opportunities, go ahead and tell them. Type Ones are not afraid to push each other to be more productive if you provide them with the proper motivation and challenges.

Type Twos. The pending acquisition has shaken your Type Two employees. They are in the early stages of depression. Each one will probably tell you he feels responsible for the acquisition and the pending changes it will impose on the organization. When you confront these employees, you have got to address their guilt and dispel any responsibility they feel. If you can successfully dispel their self-imposed guilt, you have a chance of restoring their motivation, their faith in themselves, and the company by addressing the positive aspects of the acquisition.

Type Threes. When you talk to a Type Three employee, you find that he's got a series of calculations on his BlackBerry showing how the acquisition can be accomplished without requiring his participation in the changes. Type Threes want to feel good all the time and clearly the potential acquisition is not sitting well with them. They like to operate in a self-serving environment where it is often difficult to tell whether they are the manipulator or the manipulated. They are shrewd actors and can play either role with equal finesse.

The quickest way to get the attention of your Type Three employee is to tell him when the acquisition will happen and the changes he must be prepared to address. If you cannot provide him with a target date, his insecurity will continue to grow to the point where his motivation will disappear. Assure him that you will disclose the date as soon as your superiors allow you to do so.

Type Fours. Type Fours look like they are always having fun regardless of adverse situations. When you meet with a Type Four employee, she may be full of jokes about the pending acquisition. However, Type Fours tend to be highly insecure people. The fact that the company's pending acquisition was published in this morning's paper does not sit well with your employee. As she tells you, "I've got a lot of explaining to do to my friends. What am I going to tell them?"

Type Fours are uncommitted individuals by nature. Chances are that every one of your Type Four employees updated their resume within one minute of reading the announcement in this morning's paper. They will leave you the moment they find a comparable job. If you're looking for voluntary attrition, your Type Fours will help out. If you have key Type Four employees you don't want to lose, meet with them privately to assure them that they are not on your layoff list.

CONFRONTING FINANCIAL PROBLEMS

A highly regarded systems engineer at Hewlett Packard once said to me, "The life cycle of a product around here is less than six months, and if I can't keep up with the pace, I'll be a virtual antique before I reach forty. Today's skills, knowledge, and products live fast lives and die young. We are all being asked to learn on the fly and produce more with less money at a laser-fast pace that will continue to accelerate. Change is happening faster than we can keep tabs on it."

No organization is exempt from rapid change these days, and that change as well as challenges to the financial health of an organization can have a significant impact on its employees. Sharing information from the company's income statement with the rank and file can prove to be a powerful tool if upper management is careful to share it properly and put the numbers in context so that employees understand them. However, if the numbers cause confusion, they can backfire and create significant confrontations.

The Situation

"We don't have passion in this company anymore. Instead of passion, we have bottom-line idiots, bean counters who have replaced entrepreneurs. They've crippled our research and development effort and everyone's motivation to work in the process. Now that I have said my piece, are you going to fire me?"

You ask Art, one of your most valuable employees, to sit down so that you can explain to him what's happening. This will not be an easy sell because upper management is, in fact, not running the company to your satisfaction.

Type Ones. If Art's a Type One, you don't need to spend a lot of time with him; confirm to him that the bean counters are indeed in charge and hence, their bottom-line wishes must be carried out. Tell Art to stick around awhile because they may be serving bean soup in the cafeteria in the near future. When he asks you what you mean, just smile and ask him to be patient with the company hierarchy. The issue will work itself out! He will know what you mean.

Type Twos. Art's comments demonstrate the unforgiving aspect of a Type Two's personality. You need to convince him to back off in the interest of protecting his job. If the bean counters get wind of his attitude, he's history. Ask him to be patient because adverse bottom-line situations tend to get resolved in the short term.

Type Threes. Normally, Type Threes are very patient individuals. If Art is a Type Three and has exploded in this way, he is abnormally upset. Calm him down by explaining the reality of the situation. He'll quickly come back to his senses and will be willing to wait until the bottom-line issues have been resolved. Use his natural tendency toward patience to get him back to his center.

Type Fours. Type Fours are afraid of adverse facts that could disrupt their belief that everything in life should be an enjoyable experience. Art, a Type Four, is panicking, and it's coming out as anger at upper management. Convince him that sometimes it is best to know what the facts are today so that you have the option of improving them tomorrow. Remind Art that the belt tightening that he's willing to accept today will help assure him of a better tomorrow. For a start, he'll get to keep his job.

CONFRONTING LAYOFFS

Some problems have no painless solutions, and managing a layoff is one of them. It has long been an axiom of American business that when sales or profits decline, the first element of cost that gets reduced is labor. Labor usually translates into the lowest-paid employees. In instances where drastic cutbacks are needed, it includes white-collar workers, which were traditionally not included in the cutback formula. In recent years, all of that has changed and no worker is immune, including the CEO.

It reminds me of my first job shortly after I graduated from college when the personnel manager invited me to a meeting that evening with the night shift. At the appointed time, he told 200 assembly workers that, effective immediately, they were laid off. There were tears and panic as these people tried to sort out their alternatives. In retrospect, I now understand why the personnel manger had invited me to the meeting. I was being groomed for a management position where I would be expected to exercise layoffs as they were needed by the organization.

The Situation

Your company is considering a 10 percent across the board reduction in its workforce. The announcement has appeared in this morning's newspaper, which was the first time you heard about it. When you arrive at work, you find your office flooded with employees, all demanding to know what's going on!

George jumps up and aggressively confronts you with question that you would like to avoid: "Is there any truth to the hall talk we're hearing about layoffs? We want to know if we're all going to lose our jobs."

You know there is some truth to the rumors, although nothing has come down through the official channels yet. Financially, the company is not doing as well as Wall Street would like, and you have sensed mounting pressure to reduce costs in order to boost the bottom line. Your boss has told you to anticipate several downsizing mandates by the end of the week. Now you'll have to prepare your workers for possible job losses. How they react and how you lead them will depend, as always, on their personality types.

Type Ones. Let your information-hungry Type One employees have all of the information they need to make plans for their future. Be sure to distinguish between what you know and what is merely rumored. For example, if the company is planning to announce layoffs on July 1, you have a firm date to present to them. If the magnitude of the layoffs is undecided, you can't provide them with any information. Reject any request to speculate.

Type Twos. The best way to combat downsizing rumors with your "analytical" Type Two employees is with the truth, which may be difficult if you are not sure what the truth is. Just because you're in the management chain does not give you access to all of the privileged information, so you may have to do some digging to find the facts. In the interim, explain to your Type Two employees the best you can what's going on, focusing on facts and figures. You might tell them: "I am aware of a potential plan to downsize the company. In recent months, the company has suffered some financial setbacks that have been publicized in the news media, which may be the source of the speculation about downsizing. Ignore the rumors because I will keep you informed as the facts are disclosed to me. In the meantime, focus on your work, which is the best job security you can have."

Type Threes. Your kind and considerate Type Three employees will not respond well to the downsizing rumors. To diffuse their immediate concerns, assure them that you will look into the situation and address the subject in your next staff meeting. Encourage them to discount any hall talk that they may encounter while you gather the facts and make sure they understand that the best job protection they can obtain is by demonstrating their own good performance and continued loyalty to the organization. Reassure your top employees that their jobs are secure and counsel them on what they need to do to maintain their current level of employment.

Type Fours. Inform your Type Four employees about the company's layoff policy to help minimize their insecurity over the situation. Special provisions such as early retirement or extended leaves of absence may have been put into place to cover the downsizing activities. Ask senior management to clearly explain the rules before you address the concerns of your Type Fours. Don't give them partial information; it will just make them more nervous. Keep them motivated and focused on their current assignments. Discourage them from participating in complaint sessions, which will only reinforce their insecurities, and tell them to concentrate on maintaining superior job performance. Take whatever steps you need to assure that they are motivated to perform well during the adversity caused to the downsizing activities.

PUTTING IT ALL TOGETHER

Disagreements, controversies, and personal clashes between two or more people cause confrontations. These human relation problems are often difficult to resolve, and for this reason you should avoid them as much as possible. Confrontations are unpleasant, are often disruptive to relationships, can be counterproductive, and can be costly to your leadership efforts. Regardless of who's right, nobody walks away from a confrontational situation as an absolute winner.

Unfortunately, confrontations are an inevitable part of human relationships. A leader knows how to manage confrontations by drawing out all of the issues so that he understands the differing perspectives of the individuals involved in the confrontation, and then moves to find common ground that everyone can endorse. Leaders bring the conflicting situations to the surface, acknowledge the feelings and views of all sides, and then direct their energy toward a shared solution whenever possible.

Coaching Attributes of the Four Personality Types

TYPE ONE	Very competitive and wants all jobs to be completed right. Direct, outspoken, and will show a high sense of urgency to help others become better players.
TYPE TWO	Pragmatic, detail-oriented, and consistent in their coaching style. Hard to dissuade once their mind is made up when they are energized by data.
TYPE THREE	Intense and passionate about their winning values. Likes to facilitate discussion and harmony to resolve team problems. Dislikes being caught off guard.
TYPE FOUR	Likes to get involved in many different team activities. Works in short, intense spurts of energy to help their team win. Always optimistic and good at reading between the lines.

CHAPTER 10

Coaching Your Team

*If you're the coach and you show your players
how to take advantage of every opportunity
that comes their way, they can't lose.*

IN TRADITIONAL MANAGEMENT, coaching revolves around a performance plan. The objective of the plan is to simply "fix" whatever was wrong with an employee by using fear to motivate them to perform better. Coaching takes on a whole new meaning when it is executed by a leader. Instead of focusing on fear and what will happen if the problem isn't fixed, leaders focus on the success that will occur once the problem is resolved. Their agenda merges personal goals for development with corporate problem-solving goals. Achieving the desired results leads to better individual satisfaction from being coached and a win for the entire team.

HOW LEADERS COACH

Good leaders help members of their team identify the unique strengths and weaknesses of their personality types to overcome problems and augment their career and work aspirations. They encourage their people to establish long-term developmental goals and coach them to create a plan for reaching those goals. At the same time, leaders are explicit about what their own goals are, and every one of their team members knows what their roles are in helping them achieve those goals. People tend to gravitate toward the aspects of their job that tie into their dreams and aspirations. By linking people's daily work to their personal goals, leaders keep their people's attention focused on what needs to be done.

Leaders are good at delegating as a way of coaching employees to accept challenging assignments that stretch their talents, rather than delegating tasks that simply get a routine job done. Challenging assignments create a positive impact on an employee's mood about their work environment. When you can successfully coach a person to go beyond their perceived abilities, they will reward you with newfound loyalty and respect. Along the way, a good coach communicates a belief in her team's potential and an expectation that her players can do their best to win. "I believe in you. I'm investing in you and I expect your best efforts." These are the words leaders often use to show their team members they care about them. As a result, leaders uphold their own high standards for performance and will feel accountable for how well they do.

COACHING NEW LEADERS

Leaders actively seek out ways to delegate greater decision-making authority and responsibility to their team members. Acting as coaches, they show them how to use their skills and talents to become leaders themselves. They are constantly working to develop the capabilities of their team members and foster self-confidence by allowing them to lead important team functions. For example, when a leader takes time off from work, he will typically assign the responsibility of running the department to a team member, rather than an outside manager.

The Situation

Monday morning finds you sitting at your desk with a cup of coffee reading Ray France's latest status report on the Harding project. As you read through the report, you're dismayed that things are not going well for the company's largest account. You're trying to follow Ray's plan to resolve the problems, but his sentences aren't clear, and you have no idea how he arrived at his conclusions. You're especially disgusted because this will be the third time this week he has told you he doesn't know what to do. Whenever you talk to Ray about the progress that he's making in resolving the problems, he always gives you his canned answer: "Everything is going to be okay. Trust me!" You don't trust him.

The vice president of marketing told you yesterday in no uncertain words that if the company loses the Harding account, heads will roll. Although she didn't say exactly which heads would roll, you are pretty sure yours will be one of them. You have therefore decided to step into the situation to coach Ray on what he needs to do to become a successful project leader.

> **Type Ones.** Ray reacts to your criticism about the dismal status of the Harding project with a dismissive attitude: "You're the boss and entitled to your opinion. I'm here to tell you I think the corrective action that I'm taking on this project is right on." His flippant comment reinforces in your mind that you're dealing with a strong Type One personality who becomes highly incensed when anyone challenges his work. You tell Ray that when you discussed the status of the project

with Mr. Harding, he told you "things were not going well." Type Ones respect factual information. If schedules were missed, show him the original schedule and the late completion dates. If he becomes critical of other employees and attempts to pass the blame onto someone else, remind him of his responsibilities as project leader and the trust that you had placed in him to get the job done, rather than on someone else.

Let Ray know that you are on his side and compliment him on what he has done right. However, do not back down on your original position that his overall work is not acceptable to you, but let him know you have confidence that he can perform to your work standards. Coach him on what specifically will constitute the successful completion of the project and make sure he is willing to take full leadership responsibility for the project. Document your agreement in writing with Ray and have him sign it to reinforce his leadership role and accountability for the successful completion of the project.

Type Twos. When you confront Ray in a private meeting and inform him of your dissatisfaction with the status of the Harding project, you are disturbed by his silence. Several minutes pass before he finally says something. When he tells you he's doing the best he can on the project and offers to turn the project over to whomever you designate, you know you're dealing with a self-righteous Type Two personality. Your challenge is to somehow restore Ray's self-confidence as a project leader. Tell Ray the specific areas of the project that are bothering you and openly seek his advice as to what action can be taken to correct the situation. Type Twos have good analytical minds. If they truly understand the problems that you are presenting, they will often come up with viable solutions. If Ray shows any signs of depression as a result of your criticism, assure him that you need him on this project. Statements like, "Ray, you are the man for this job, so let's get on with it" will go a long way toward dampening a Type Two's tendency to become depressed over something they have done wrong.

Type Threes. The Harding project is extremely important to you because you've got your job riding on the successful outcome of this project. When you explain your dissatisfaction to Ray and the way he has been handling everything, you are disturbed that he's too understanding about your concerns. He readily agrees with everything you say. You are convinced that you're dealing with a "too cooperative" Type Three personality who will say anything they think you want to hear to accommodate you. As the old expression goes, "It's time to take the bull by the horns before you get gored." Show Ray exactly what you want him to do. Work with him to develop a plan to get the project done, complete with a detailed schedule and specific definitions of completion milestones. Make absolutely certain that Ray understands what is expected of him and that he understands what needs to be done to complete each milestone. Type Threes tend to be uncommitted to anything that does not have a value to them. Ask for Ray's commitment to re-establish himself as the project's leader before you turn him loose for another try. Make sure he understands the consequences (job demotion, termination, etc.) if the project is not completed on time. Reinforce the priority of the project. It may be appropriate to offer some kind of reward to Ray when he successfully completes the project. Type Threes like recognition events for their achievements.

Type Fours. When you confront Ray and inform him of your concerns on the Harding project, he apologizes profusely about his performance. Halfway through his emotional outburst, you interrupt him and ask him when he can complete the project. When he gives you one of those puzzled looks and tells you, "I can't commit to a time frame right now," you know you're dealing with an uncommitted Type Four personality who will need a lot of coaching support.

Ray may honestly not know what is expected of him to complete the project, which is why he backed off from making a commitment to you. Coach him to create a revised and realistic completion schedule. Once you have Ray's commitment to complete the project within the time frame the two of you have established, ask him again if he believes the revised schedule is realistic. Type Fours are highly optimistic individuals. If Ray sounds too optimistic or doesn't challenge at least one part of the schedule, your guard should be up. He may be endorsing the revised schedule as the easy way out of an awkward situation. Review all aspects of the project with Ray and repeatedly ask him if he understands what needs to be done to complete the project in the time frame that you have established. Verify in your mind that he truly understands the importance of this assignment as a project leader.

COACHING EMPLOYEES TO LEARN

Learning is the process where knowledge is created through the mentoring of experience from a coach to team members who want to be more effective. Over the years, personal coaching has received a great deal of attention and a number of books have been written that show how to coach the art of learning. The fact remains that you probably have employees who are either motivated to learn more or are not motivated to learn anything. The motivated team members aren't satisfied with where they are in life and are striving to learn all they can to achieve higher goals in life. Conversely, the unmotivated are satisfied with where they are in life and are not interested in changing their status quo.

The Situation

Sally has been with the company longer than any of your other employees. She joined the company as a sales representative. Although she had no previous sales background, she possessed an innate ability and desire to learn how to sell. Over the years, she consistently met or exceeded her sales quotas. As a result, you recently promoted her to district sales manager. Since that time, several of her top sales reps have consistently missed their sales quotas. The word that's out in the hallways is that her sales staff despises her leadership style.

Initially, you thought the problem was temporary in nature and would simply go away. Sally has in the past been a good producer, anxious to learn everything she could to improve herself, and was a highly motivated individual. When you initially assessed Sally's situation, you assumed that she was probably encountering temporary personal problems that were disrupting her sales leadership abilities. You broach the subject with the CEO and he told you, "Fix whatever is causing the deterioration of our sales." You get his point and realize that the mounting concerns from upper management and Sally's own sales staff demand your immediate attention and coaching.

Type Ones. If Sally is a "take charge" individual and is trying her best to do a good job without soliciting any advice, she is probably a Type One. The fact that her sales reps are on her case bothers her a great deal. To your knowledge, she has not openly shared her concerns with anybody, which could be the major cause of her insecurity and loss of motivation to learn more about the problem. Her personality attributes indicate to you that she is hard working, likes challenges, but does not accept criticism well. However, Type Ones don't object to being coached to overcome problems if they acknowledge that they have one. In the past, Sally was always productive so there was no need to coach her in this area. For some reason, she is unable to communicate effectively with her staff, which is her main problem. It may be because this is the first time in her career that she has been a sales leader and she doesn't know what is expected of her. As a result, she is ignoring the fact that she has communication problems with her team.

Sally needs to understand what her communication problem is before you can coach her on how to overcome it. You convince her to meet on a one-on-one basis with her top sales representatives. With your prompting and coaching, she is prepared to ask each of her reps, "What can I do to improve my level of communication throughout the sales organization?" Learning about the problem is an important first step to build a recovery plan.

Type Ones like the challenge of achieving tough goals. Sally needs you to help her develop communication goals. The overall goals may be to motivate everybody on her team to welcome her leadership in helping them meet or exceed their sales quota by a specified date. Encourage Sally to attend a dynamic sales motivation seminar to help her develop her communication skills.

Have her hold follow-up meetings with her sales reps on a regular basis so that she has a way of confirming her progress. Yes, you should attend some of those meetings to confirm that you are supporting Sally. Consider adding a goal attainment incentive for the department that will excite the sales people and encourage them to support Sally.

Type Twos. From what you know about Sally, you suspect that she has a classic Type Two personality. She appears to be very sensitive to the problem and is openly upset over the fact that she has not been able to resolve her sales leadership problems, which is devastating her motivation. You hope that she is not too sensitive, in view of the pressure that is mounting on her to increase sales. In your one-on-one encounter with Sally, she reveals more insecurities than you have time to listen to. This is typical of Type Two personalities. Sally's insecurities are directly affecting her ability to learn to communicate more effectively with anybody. The key to getting her back on track will be to either eliminate or neutralize her insecurities as best that you can.

In a follow-up session with Sally, jointly prioritize all of the weak areas of her personality—most to least critical. Develop a plan to eliminate the first three weak issues on the list before you coach her on how to address her other weak areas. As you begin to help Sally resolve key insecurity issues, monitor the way she communicates with her staff. Her level of communication should dramatically improve as she becomes more secure in what she's doing. Offer her an opportunity to attend a communication seminar to reinforce the fact that you care about her. Joint weekly meetings would be in order where the two of you can review the progress she's making at resolving her weak areas of performance.

Type Threes. In view of the fact that Sally's performance is unsatisfactory, you ask her to confidentially discuss her understanding of the problem with you. She tells you, "As I stated earlier, our sales quotas are determined from the strategic planning numbers that marketing prepares, which, of course, are bogus numbers." Based on Sally's presentation, you are convinced that she has a Type Three personality because she did not address any of the problems she is encountering with her sales reps.

Type Threes will do anything they can to bypass or ignore major problems, and can be difficult to read. They'll often oversimplify a problem to the point where you may believe they are completely unaware of what's going on. In most cases, Type Threes are acutely aware of the situation and will hide their real feelings of inadequacy. You need to get Sally to openly address her problems with you. If she will not do this, you'll never be able to coach her to solve her communication problems with her sales team. If Sally refuses to acknowledge the problem, try this scenario: "Sally, you and I are both aware of the fact that sales are down significantly. I need you to *help* me solve our problem." Appeal to Sally's need to overcome depression by emphasizing the word "help" and your willingness to play an active role as her coach.

Type Fours. You catch Sally in the hallway and ask her how things are going. She tells you, "Our sales performance this year is not good. Some of our top sales reps missed their quotas by as much as 50 percent." You ask her, "What were the reasons for the wide fluctuations and variances in sales?" After some deliberation, a hurt look appears on her face. She gives you a rebellious reply: "Listen, I'm doing the best I can. I'm hampered by poor upper management." You have part of the answer that you were looking for—Sally has a Type Four personality whose feelings are very easily hurt, which can cause her to offer vague excuses rather than addressing the real problem. Apply different coaching tactics to get her back on track.

Type Fours like to bound through life having fun and frequently will consider their job a "necessary evil." It's required because they need the money to buy the fun things they enjoy. Sally performed well on the job as long as it was relatively easy for her to meet her sales quota. When she became sales manager, she wasn't willing to make the personal sacrifices to work harder to keep her sales team on track. You need to point this out to her and get her to commit to a stronger work ethic. Offer her an opportunity to attend a "work smart" seminar to learn more about what it takes be a sales leader. Do not be afraid to remind Type Fours that we all like to play, but that it takes money (i.e., a good job) to play the really fun games. Encourage and even demand that she reorganize her priorities—job first and personal fun second.

COACHING ACCOUNTABILITY

When Andy Gere was appointed to the new position of water treatment manager at San Jose Water Company, an investor-owned water utility service in Silicon Valley, his challenge was to transform a fragmented, feuding group of managers into a cohesive, cooperative workforce. With Andy's leadership and coaching, they developed a set of guidelines for communicating and solving problems as a team. The guidelines were published in a manual called *An Operator's Guide to Making Teamwork Work*. All executives of the company signed an agreement that made the guidelines a contract for the way they would work with one another. Accountability was pushed by reminding the players to focus on the problem as a team, making each accountable to the success of the company.

The Situation

The accountability for financial problems can be disturbing in any organization. The natural tendency is for everyone to avoid ownership—even at times when the numbers (i.e., dollars) are their responsibility. Often people will undermine a course of action that requires change by ridiculing it.

All of your attempts to resolve the escalating costs that have permeated your production department have gone nowhere. When you attended the monthly management meeting, you were irritated at the comments some of the managers directed to Meg Reagan, your production supervisor, who presented several viable solutions to the problem. Meg left the meeting dispirited. You sense from the comments that were made by managers in the meeting that they do not believe she is capable of carrying out any of the cost-reduction plans she presented.

The loss of a person's credibility can devastate their career. You believe one of Meg's plans was right on the mark and could save the company millions. Her idea to shorten the time it takes to process Internet orders by 75 percent would drop costs dramatically and customer satisfaction would definitely improve.

The implementation of her Internet order-processing idea will require the participation and accountability of several department heads. You decide to coach her on how to get people to become accountable and endorse her ideas.

Type Ones. If Meg is a Type One, she may have been too assertive and self-serving when she presented her Internet idea. Coach her on accountability techniques (i.e., who owns what part of the plan, etc.) she can use to encourage others to participate and help implement her plan. Work with her to develop an interdepartmental implementation schedule that clearly identifies who is accountable for what parts of the plan. Coach her on techniques she can use to solicit the participants to help her develop the plan. Once she has identified her team members, focus her attention on getting the team to agree on the goals and objectives of the program.

Type Twos. If Meg has a detail-oriented Type Two personality, she can become highly suspicious of anyone who challenges her ideas. Ask her to explain to you the specifics of the Internet order-entry changes that she would like to implement and why she believes they will be successful. Listen intently to what she has to say, affirm your confidence in her plan, and address every issue that Meg brings up.

Before you sign off on the plan, encourage her to accept viable ideas from other department members who will be affected by it. Type Twos want to be assured that all of the variables are covered, so she should comply with your suggestion. Once Meg has the organization's commitment and willingness to be accountable for the plan, you can count on Meg's leadership to see the project through to completion.

Type Threes. If Meg has a Type Three personality, she may have second thoughts about implementing the Internet idea that she presented at the managers' meeting. Type Threes can become reluctant to take any action when they face peer pressure. Remind her of all the compelling reasons for implementing the change. Coach Meg on how to work with and solicit support from the organization for buy-in and accountability. Encourage her to incorporate their viable ideas in her implementation plan and give them credit for it. Type Threes are not opposed to changes that clearly benefit the organization.

Your help and coaching will build Meg's trust in you so that you can continue making suggestions for its successful implementation.

Type Fours. If Meg is a Type four, she will want 100 percent of your approval for her plan before she will even attempt to implement it. Listen carefully to her reasons for wanting to implement the new Internet order-entry system and actively make suggestions to her. Impress upon her the importance that she gets management endorsement and help her identify the potential causes for their resistance. Work with her on a strategy to eliminate their resistance as quickly as possible. Be frank in your discussion with her and let her know exactly what you think of her ideas and coach her on how she can improve the implementation part of her plan. If she agrees with you, make sure it's a sincere answer because Type Fours are not afraid to give an answer that they think you want to hear just to satisfy you.

If Meg tells you she does not want to implement the new Internet system, be patient, and ask her why she has changed her mind. If she gives you a reason that you can do something about, like extending the end date for the change, ask her if you did that, would she implement the system? If she gives you a nebulous response that implies that she just wants to give up, coach her to continue moving forward and not backward, which Type Fours will often try to do.

COACHING CHANGE

I used to be a subscriber to the philosophy, "If it isn't broke, don't fix it," until somebody gave me a copy of Robert Kriegel's book *If It Ain't Broke . . . Break It!* I used to think, why work on something that's working when you can work on plenty of other stuff that is not working. However, the one thing we can count on is that rip-roaring changes are already challenging everything we do today and are shaking the foundations of the world around us. Changes in work styles, economic conditions, technology, corporate structures, global competition, lifestyles, and environmental challenges are happening at the speed of light. In the past, change occurred incrementally and at a slower pace. We had the luxury of first debating if we wanted to change, and then methodically planning how we would implement the change at whatever pace we chose. Not any more!

To keep on top of changes and the opportunities they present, you need to adopt a whole new way of thinking in your coaching style, one that is a radical departure from the past. If you stick with a "what's working today" mentality, you will not only miss out on opportunities, but you'll find yourself struggling to maintain obsolete systems that demand to be changed. A fundamental change in thinking is needed that is as radical as the pace of today's change. If you expect to compete in today's changing world, coach your people to fix something while it's still working to make it better or replace it with something that's already better. If you wait until it's broke, it will be too late to fix it!

The Situation

Your good friend and associate, Dan Nelsen, walks into your office and slams the door. You can tell he's upset about something. He says, "After that 'if it ain't broke, break it, and fix it' meeting this morning, I spent some time roaming the hallways and hanging around the water coolers. I did a lot of listening and talking to the employees. I'm here to tell you that the word is out on this change everything program employees are referring to as the 'fix it' program. They're excited about the concept and can't wait to participate in the program. However, there is some serious opposition that you need to be aware of as well. Several members of your staff are concerned about what will happen if some of the new ways of doing things run counter to their beliefs. For instance, your operations supervisor, Tim Doughtfire, will do everything he can to block any change his team members suggest. As I see it, you're in a lose-lose situation."

You begin your Monday morning staff meeting with an opening remark: "I know the decision to move more of the operational decision-making responsibilities down to the employees through the new 'fix it' program will not be an easy one to implement. But given today's productivity challenges, we have got no choice if we want to stay competitive. Does anybody have any comments or thoughts that they would like to make on the subject?"

The expected confrontation from Tim Doughtfire begins as soon as he stands up and says, "Quite frankly, I am concerned about our ability to pull this employee 'fix it' thing off. The whole program runs counter to our basic management philosophy that fixing something is management's responsibility, not something to be delegated down to the rank and file."

As you listen to the rest of what Tim says, you can't help thinking to yourself that he is the most underempowered "won't change" person you have on your staff. A flashlight battery has more changing power than this man. What can you do to get him to join you in this self-improvement program? You decide to stretch your personal coaching talents and get him to endorse this change.

Type Ones. Type Ones are generally receptive to change at work and are future oriented. If Tim is a Type One, there may be something in his personal life that is causing him to not support the "fix it" program. A private conversation and coaching session outside of the work place is in order with him. Take him out to lunch and diplomatically express your concerns about his lack of support. Ask him if there is any work-related issue that is bothering him. If not, try to find out what personal issues are bothering him that you could help him resolve. Remind him that employee satisfaction is crucial in retaining lower-level employees and reducing turnover costs.

Type Twos. If Tim has a Type Two personality, he is a focused individual who has the innate ability to concentrate on whatever demands his attention in any given situation. When he's at work, he should be able to focus on the task at hand in an organized frame of mind. The fact is, he may not be motivated to take on anything else like the "fix it" program because of his current workload. Confront Tim about the situation and honestly express your concerns. Chances are, there is some work that you can reprioritize for him to get him back on track to support the "fix it" program.

Type Threes. Type Threes can quickly become uncommitted to anything that they don't believe in, including the "fix it" program. If Tim is a Type Three, he can go from an active team player to an inactive team player overnight. You'll find yourself asking the question, "What happened to Tim? Yesterday he was full of motivation and today he looks like he's been zapped by a de-motivator machine!" Approach Tim and ask him why he's not committed to the program? If he gives you an answer that he is comfortable in his routine work environment and is resistant to implementing changes, put together a coaching initiative to help him understand why changes are needed. Encourage him to get positive feedback from his employees on changes that he has made to help build his self-esteem.

Type Fours. While some Type Fours find change exciting, many are uncomfortable with change and even consider it threatening if they fear that it might disrupt their work environment. If this is the case with Tim, he will have a variety of different reasons for not wanting to participate in new programs. Listen carefully to what he says when you ask him why he doesn't want to be a part of the "fix it" program. Identify the cause of his resistance and coach him on how to eliminate them as quickly as possible.

COACHING TEAM REJECTS

The popularity and growth of teams that are organized to solve specific problems or issues (usually short-term ones) has been phenomenal. Managers boast of the number of teams they have organized, the problems they have solved with teams, and how much money teams have saved the company. One of the most important considerations in team effectiveness is the relationship team members have with their team leader. To become viable, team leaders must be able to adjust their behavior to adapt to the personalities of the team members. If they can't do that, the team's mission may not be accomplished. Teamwork is accomplished by making cooperative and mutual respect a critical component of the team's mindset. An outstanding leader is constantly developing new and dynamic coaching techniques for their team.

The Situation

You can't refrain from thinking that Karen, one of your newest employees, is a "team reject." For some reason, Karen is the laughingstock of every team you've put her on. Even after the team assignment ends, Karen continues to demonstrate the same inflexible and judgmental attitude to anybody she talks to. In addition, she voices negative comments to her associates, which causes recurring conflicts. Your peer managers have picked up on the situation, and when one of them confronts you in the cafeteria with a smirk on his face and asks sarcastically if he can borrow Karen to head up his next team, you decide to coach Karen on how to become a team player.

Type Ones. Because of Karen's arrogant attitude, you believe she has a Type One personality. She does not seem to fit in well with any team and has an innate ability to turn off team members. This is unfortunate since well-functioning Type Ones tend to exert loyalty and support from team members. Counsel Karen on techniques she can use to control her arrogance. Suggest to her that she spend more time listening to team discussions before she renders her ideas and opinions on the subject being discussed. To be successful, every team member must be a source of positive reinforcement for the other team members, a role that Karen is clearly not fulfilling. Coach her on how to support other team members and separate her private opinions from those interactions.

Type Twos. If Karen is a Type Two, she may be too analytical when given a team assignment. When she perpetually asks what's the problem that the team is trying to solve, recognize that she is searching for answers that may not have been discovered by the team—in fact, the team's mission may be to define the problem. Unfortunately, her analytical questions may be delaying rather than advancing the team objective. She would rather continually define and redefine the problem than work on the solution. The team members recognize this fact and reluctantly allow her to pursue her search for a finite definition, while the rest of the team works on the solution to the problem. This issue needs to be brought to Karen's attention before you can motivate her to function effectively in a team environment. She needs to understand her problem before you can coach her on a solution.

Type Threes. If Karen is a Type Three, she likes to work in environments that are free of peer pressure. Some problems are better solved by people working alone on one or more tasks. Karen may be a greater asset to the team working autonomously than in a group setting. This is a more comfortable role for many Type Threes. Coach Karen on the techniques she can use to present her good ideas in a manner that supports what the team wants to accomplish.

Type Fours. If Karen has a Type Four personality, she is uncomfortable with how teams with specific assignments fit into the organization. Point out that as a team member she is responsible for sharing information with her team members that will help the team achieve the goal that has been assigned to it. Tell her that if she does not actively participate in team discussions, that may be perceived by the other team members as reflecting a lack of interest in the team. You must coach Karen on how to present her ideas in a manner that is constructive to the overall efforts of the team.

PUTTING IT ALL TOGETHER

Broadcaster Paul Harvey once said, "In tough times like these it is good to remember that there have always been tough times like these." No leader can simultaneously have his head buried in the sand and see his way clear to coach people through tough times. If you're a coach your organization is counting on, you had better know how to teach everybody on your team how to survive when they run into tough times or you won't be a coach for long. There are going to be times when your best plans are going to become a victim of someone who works for you. How you rise up to meet that challenge and apply the attributes of the person's personality to resolve their problems will determine your level of greatness as a coach.

Measure your success not only by the tough problems you've solved today, but by tough problems you solved yesterday. Ask questions as you're coaching and activate your listening capability along with your peripheral vision. In the process, you'll get better at the art of coaching as you gain experience dealing with the members of your team and organization. Actively look for tough situations that need fixing, apply your coaching prowess to fix them, and then go to the next problem on a priority basis.

PART III

Your Career as a Leader

THE CAREER OF leaders develops naturally with an organization. In the workplace, you will often see them managing the diversity of any group they come in contact with. They have the innate ability to communicate with clarity, facilitate problem solving, and engender a feeling of service to a larger cause that inspires and motivates those they're talking to.

Far too often we think of larger career causes, as it were, some benchmark serving a higher religious, social, or humane cause rather than an immediate "people needs" cause. Effective leaders know how to move their career ambitions down into the everyday operation of their organization because that is where the action is. When team leaders help their fellow workers replace statements like "That's not my job or my fault" with "What can I do to help?" their career as a team leader is established forever in the organization they work for.

Persuasive Attributes of the Personality Types

TYPE ONE	They are task oriented individuals who respond well to direct persuasive tactics that appeal to what they think is important.
TYPE TWO	They are people-oriented and creative individuals who respond well to persuasive tactics that address people issues.
TYPE THREE	They like to be free of pressure and are adaptable to persuasive ideas that are popular with their peers.
TYPE FOUR	They are self-serving individuals who respond well to persuasive tactics that encourage them to commit to something that is good for them.

CHAPTER 11

Persuading Your Peers

*The true measure of leaders is their ability
to persuade people to follow them.*

IN THE UNIVERSITIES of Europe during the Middle Ages, persuasion (usually termed "rhetoric") was one of the seven liberal arts to be mastered by any educated man. From the days of imperial Rome through the Reformation, it was raised to a fine art by preachers who used the spoken word to inspire actions ranging from virtuous behavior to religious pilgrimages. In the modern era, persuasion is most visible in the form of commercial advertisements.

In previous chapters, we've discussed how to motivate your employees and how to weld the different personalities into a single, well-functioning team. In this section, we turn to your relationships with your colleagues, those at work who are managers striving to be leaders. The persuasion techniques that we address in this chapter are ones you can employ to motivate and inspire your peers, persuading them to do what you want them to do. The different situations that we present cast you into a range of scenarios from resolving hostile peer relationships to soliciting other managers' support.

The ability to effectively persuade peers is essential for anyone who wants to move up the leadership ladder. Persuasive leaders are the ones others gladly follow and are easy to recognize in any group setting. If the group is trying to decide on an issue, who is the person to whom they turn for an opinion? Who is the one they eventually agree with? People rely on persuasive leaders.

Robert Dilenschneider is one of the best persuasive leaders in the country. He's the CEO of Hill and Knowlton, an international public relations firm. He knows how to skillfully weave his persuasive magic into the international business arena where megacorporations meet to fight over who gets what out of the world's economy. In his book, *Power and Influence*, he discusses three persuasion components that are essential: communication, benefits, and justification. Let's explore how each of these components works to persuade the different personality types.

PERSUADING WITH COMMUNICATION

The art of persuading others is in many respects, a communication game. The better you're able sell ideas with your words, the more people will think of you as a contributor to the organization. It's easy when they agree with you. It's when they disagree with you that things can get tough. If that happens, explore the reasons for their objections and carefully listen to what they have to say. We all have a tendency to offer an immediate answer to an objection just to get it out of the way. When you do that, often the person making the objection stops listening. She's too busy thinking about what else she can say to buttress her objection.

Ask a lot of probing questions when you're attempting to persuade someone. Using questions to get the answers you need is an important tool in the overall persuasion process. When asking a question, explain why you're asking it. If a question stands alone, it may raise another question in the listener's mind. The more that you can learn about how a person is thinking, the better you will be able to adjust your persuasion techniques to fit the situation.

One of the biggest inhibitors to clear communication is the lack of sincerity by the person you're trying to persuade. If you do not believe you are getting straight answers from the other person, you will get nowhere. The need to get people to tell you the truth can be a difficult challenge, particularly if they don't like or respect you. Lack of sincerity is often evident in a person's facial and body inflections. A tight smile or a rapid movement of her arms while she talks in a tense voice might indicate to you that you're not getting her real opinions.

The Situation

"I like being direct," you say to Glen as you enter his office and shut the door. In fact, you've had conflicting differences with Glen for some time now. You are acutely aware of the fact that he has been sabotaging your effort to consolidate two of your departments into one group, and you cannot understand why. Your objective in this morning's meeting is to find out why he's doing it, and this time you want the truth so that you can persuade him to endorse your position.

Type Ones. If Glen is a Type One, he can be an insensitive and calculating individual who must be handled with all the care you would give to a rattlesnake. Glen's caustic remarks behind your back about your attempt to consolidate two departments demonstrate this personality attribute. The only way to get Glen's honest opinion is to buy it. Promise him something that he wants in return for his support (e.g., your support for one of his goals, an open-ended IOU, etc.).

Type Twos. As a Type Two, Glen likes people. This places you in an advantageous position to find out why he's sabotaging your consolidation efforts. Use humor to put him in a relaxed mood. Then ask him for his honest (stress the word honest) reasons for not supporting you. It's important that you understand his reasons first, before you attempt to persuade him. If he avoids looking at you when he answers a question, he may not be telling you the truth.

Type Threes. Type Threes can be very unforgiving if they believe you have crossed them. Whatever you have done to Glen, he clearly doesn't like you if he is sabotaging your consolidation effort behind your back. Whatever he tells you, it will be a lie unless you can direct his attention at something he does cares about. Your approach might be, "Glen, although our relationship has not been good, I need to get your opinion on something, not for myself but for . . ." Now include something he cares about: a person, a project, a bonus. Type Threes are notorious for dodging difficult questions that they don't want to answer honestly.

Type Fours. Type Fours can be extremely obnoxious people who think it is clever to not tell the truth when someone needs their support. The only way to get Type Four Glen to be honest with you is to convince him of the seriousness of what you're trying to accomplish with your consolidation plan. Ask him if he will give you straight answers to the questions that you would like to ask him. Listen carefully to his answer to determine, as best you can, if he will be honest with you. Then ask him, "Why aren't you supporting my consolidation plan?" Listen carefully to what he has to say. Contorted facial expressions are a classic Type Four indicator that they're not telling you the truth.

PERSUADING WITH BENEFITS

If you want to sell your ideas, never suggest an action without stating its benefit. Before you attempt to sell any idea, think about all of the benefits it will bring to the table, and suggest them in ascending order of importance. Save your best benefits for the last and only use them if they are needed. For example, suppose you say to your colleague, "I would like to work on the Harding Project." That's the idea you want to sell, but now you must offer him a benefit. You add, "I can then leverage the excellent relationship that I have with our CEO to get this project back on the right track. He trusts me. And that'll make us both look good." The Harding Project is a major effort to escalate employee productivity throughout the organization by 20 percent. Your colleague agrees with your suggestion and suggests you work with another peer, Tim, in Human Relations, to come up with a viable plan that will get the project back on schedule. Your challenge will be to convince Tim to adopt a softer approach to employee relations so that viable motivational tactics can be applied to improve employee productivity.

The Situation

Tim is a big man. You guess he probably played football in high school or college, and got into HR by accident. Before joining the company three years ago, he managed a chain of "hard nose" credit and collection offices. You walk into Tim's office for your planned meeting. Tim starts the conversation off on an aggressive note when you ask him what he thinks about your working on the Harding Project.

"As director of operations," he says, "it's my job to make sure the company gets its worth out of everyone who works here. Let's face it, with the exception of some managers, most people fall into a pattern."

He continues, "In my opinion, the average employee nowadays has an inherent dislike for work. You just can't motivate them. Employees have to be coerced and threatened to get them to put forth adequate effort toward achieving the company's objectives. Most employees want to avoid responsibility and want to be directed. They have relatively little ambition, but they do want job security. We can use the job security issue to our advantage and bolster productivity. What do you think?" You look at the year on your notebook calendar to verify that you are in fact operating in the twenty-first and not the early twentieth century. "Tim," you say, "your outlook on human relations has been, to say the least, enlightening." Tim beams with his perception of what he thinks is a compliment. You then ask him, "What kind of employee turnover rates are we experiencing annually?"

After rummaging through his notes, Tim gives you a number that sends you to the floor: 25 to 30 percent. "Isn't that high and an indication of low employee morale?"

Tim gives you the answer that you were afraid of hearing: "Yes, but it allows us to hire replacements at cheaper rates than we were paying the ones who quit. Most of the quitters were dissenters anyway, so it's no great loss." What can you do to persuade Tim to adapt a more humanistic approach?

Type Ones. Type Ones believe it's their way or the highway. They are demanding and very critical of others. Type Ones are impatient with human inadequacy and feel that nothing short of efficiency should be tolerated. Type Ones respond to incentives, so make sure you can identify the benefits of your program that will accomplish what you want—increased productivity using motivational tactics instead of orders. Show Tim how these benefits outweigh those offered by his system, and he'll respond favorably.

Type Twos. If Type Twos judge your intended actions to be wrong, they will do everything in their power to disrupt your efforts. You won't be able to motivate Tim to change his behavior if he will not buy into your program. As a Type Two, Tim is also greedy for details and analysis. Have lots of facts and figures with you. Be patient and be willing to review your plan complete with all its benefits.

Type Threes and Fours. In the above example, Tim showed himself to be a power monger of the worst type. It is highly unlikely that you will have to deal with a Type Three or Four power monger since that feature is not inherent in their personality types. However, watch out for the exception. Type Threes and Type Fours can become power mongers if they have a sponsor such as an associate or close personal friend who is higher up in the organization. They will parrot whatever you say that they don't like or disclose actions that you take that they don't like to their sponsor. Although Type Threes and Fours are typically loyal to their leader, they can get off track with their leader. A reorientation discussion is in order to remind and reinforce to them that you're in charge of their team. Do not use threatening words. Offer them an opportunity to leave your team if, for any reason, they do not want to accept your terms. In most cases, they will want to remain on your team.

PERSUADING WITH JUSTIFICATION

Let's assume that you are attempting to persuade an associate to support a product price recommendation that you're about to make. You have done an excellent job of choosing the right words to communicate what you want to do. The benefits that you outlined were great. Now, what is the final step in the persuasion process? Your justification, showing why it is the right thing to do and why it is the right business decision to make. When you make a concluding statement about an idea, state why you think it is justified. If you use justification as the basis of your conclusion, you will increase your credibility and chances of persuading the people you're talking to. Recognize that people can be skeptical if they don't know how you drew your conclusions. They subsequently may doubt your justification.

To negate this problem, you might say, "Based on the numbers that I have shown you, I believe that it would be appropriate to implement my idea. What do you think?" By adding the "What do you think" question, you offer an opportunity to either agree or disagree with the basis of your conclusion and justification. If they disagree, at least you have gained the advantage of knowing if they have an objection so that you can respond accordingly.

Justification within an organization is like the temperature within a body. As long as the temperature is still warm, the body is still alive and presumably functioning. As long as there is justification in the organization, there is a reason for it to exist. It gives employees a direction for what they are supposed to be doing such as searching for the best possible solutions to problems. For example, if a major flaw is suddenly discovered in a product that is critical to the success of the organization, every employee will be motivated to resolve the problem. Their justification for doing so is their concern over losing their job if the organization were to go out of business.

However, conflict between peers can quickly develop over what may be and may not be justified in their minds.

The Situation

Let's imagine you propose to your colleagues a 10 percent across the board price increase in all home plumbing hardware products. You conclude your presentation with what you think is a "no brainer" justification: "This price increase makes good business sense." But looking at the different types of personalities in the room, you realize that to persuade them you must offer justifications for the proposal that are tailored to their types.

Type Ones. The dominant operating style of Type Ones will often cause personal conflicts between you and them. Because they think they are always right, they will have a difficult time accepting your opinions unless you take advantage of their need for quantifiable facts. Provide them with a justification that clearly shows the cost versus revenue dollars before and after the proposed price increase.

Type Twos. Type Twos must have a solid reason in their minds before they will accept a major change like your proposed price increase. Although they will be interested in the numbers that you showed their Type One peers, they will want to know how this change will affect the long-term outlook of the organization. How will it affect the company's competitive position? What impact will it have on consumer sales demand? Type Twos are highly analytical and detail-oriented. Make sure these issues are covered in your justification.

Type Threes. The stubborn nature of Type Threes will often cause conflicts with their peers. Type Threes are not easy to upset so don't underestimate the issues that may underlie their conflict with your proposed price increase idea. Play on their pleasant nature to open up a dialog so that you can find out what they need to know. Encourage them to speak and to ask questions so that you can incorporate their concerns into your justification position.

Type Fours. Type Fours generally don't like conflict—particularly with peers. If they are reluctant to endorse your price increase idea, ask carefully worded probing questions to find out the reasons for their reluctance. For example, you might ask; "If you were me, what approach would you take to justify the price increase?" Remember, Type Fours do not like to express their thoughts on complex subjects unless they are asked. They also like to see immediate benefits for themselves and don't enjoy involving themselves in a lot of boring detail.

PERSUADING FOR SUPPORT

In the previous section, we showed you how to use Dilenschneider's persuasion components (communication, benefits, and justification) to help you persuade your peers. Now, let's discuss other techniques you can use when you have a specific need for support, advice, or cooperation that you are attempting to get from a peer.

Forbes magazine's recent annual corporate survey showed that 90 percent of the companies admitted that their management programs left a lot to be desired when it came to building support across departmental boundaries. One of the exceptions was Tassani Communications where managers are encouraged to spend time with other managers on a recurring basis. Managers are given the option of selecting a peer manager to shadow or an executive picks one for them. In either event, the objective is the same—follow one of your peers about for a day to learn what he does to broaden your perspective. It's a great way to get everybody in the company involved in training, it doesn't cost a lot of money for the program, and it encourages support between managers.

The Situation

You are part of the marketing department and have just been given an assignment to spearhead the introduction of a new product that your company has developed. You're acutely aware of the fact that many of your peers consider marketing as an unnecessary function. You're tired of hearing them accusing you of always trying to sell something nobody wants. If you can figure out a way to gain your peers' support to help you introduce this new product successfully, you will be in line for a promotion.

Roy Gordon, who is fondly called "Flash Gordon" within the product development ranks of the company, is a short, stocky man who always seems to bristle with enthusiasm. Over the past five years, the company has gone through four product development managers. Roy was hired away from a major competitor nine months ago and is the newest member of the management team. His department developed the product that you have been assigned to introduce into the market, and he has no use for marketing. You don't know anything about the technical features of the product. Roy has the technical knowledge you desperately need to assure its successful market introduction. How are you going to be able to persuade Roy to support your marketing effort?

You have scheduled an informal meeting with Roy under the guise that you are interested in learning how new products are developed. As you enter Roy's office, he greets you with an energetic "Welcome to my office and I hope you are having a good day."

You are not having a good day, but you manage to smile anyway. Before you can even sit down, he starts his presentation: "As you can see, Exhibit 1 on the board is a flow chart that shows how our company analyzes and develops new products. Ideas for new products can come from any department, but all ideas are carefully screened by my engineers to determine if they are viable and offer sales opportunities for the company. Notice that I used the word 'sales' rather than 'marketing' in front of the word 'opportunities.' That's because I believe the action is in Sales and not Marketing, which is a waste of time and money."

What can you do to solicit Roy's support?

Type Ones. You can have a healthy relationship with a Type One if it's built on a friendship between you and him. During the course of your conversation with Roy, look for things that are of common interest to the two of you. For example, if you both like to fish, suggest a fishing trip in order to help earn Roy's friendship. If you can develop a friendship with Roy, you will be rewarded with his undying support and assistance in introducing new products into the market.

Type Ones like to exercise their power and influence within an organization. If, when you're presenting your case to Roy, you refer to it as *his product*, the support that you need from him will fall into place. Type Ones wants to be the leader in everything they do, so let Roy think he's the leader of your market introduction project.

Type Twos. You manage to catch Roy having lunch by himself in the cafeteria and ask if you can join him. After several minutes of meaningless conversation about the weather, you ask him a question that has been nagging you. "Roy, do you involve any of the other departments in the product development process? For example, do our finance and accounting people review your production cost numbers? Is any market research done by our marketing department to test the market potential of new products that are under consideration? Does the sales organization participate in the pricing analysis?" Roy tells you, "I actively solicit support from any department that can contribute to the successful introduction of a new product. I'm a team player, always have been and always will be." Roy told you what you wanted to know. He's got a team-playing Type Two personality.

Type Twos value intimacy. If you present Roy with a list of concerns you have relative to new product introduction, he will go out of his way to offer advice and any resources he has to help you resolve problems, as long as he trusts you. Type Twos consider themselves to be morally good people. If you lie or deceive Roy, he will cut you out of his communication channel and, if given the chance, do anything he can to discredit you. But if you get him on your team, he'll be loyal to you.

Type Threes. By chance, you happen to attend a meeting where there is a confrontation between a sales manager and Roy. The sales manager registers his dissatisfaction of Roy's newest product line, which apparently is not meeting expectations. In a demanding voice, he asks, "Roy, why don't you show the sales figures for the last ten products that your group has introduced? That will give us an indication of how unsuccessful you've been at developing marketable products." Without showing any emotion, Roy tells the sales manager, "You're entitled to your opinion," and abruptly leaves the room. It's clear Roy wants to be understood and appreciated. It's equally clear that a confrontation with the sales manager would not have accomplished his Type Three desire to please others.

Type Threes like to be respected. Tell Roy you are on his side and that the sales manager was wrong. That simple statement may be all that you need to do to earn Roy's trust, support, and help for your market introduction program. Type Threes like security. Tell Roy he'll get partial credit for the successful market introduction of the new product, which will go a long ways toward solidifying a positive relationship with him.

Type Fours. Based on the research you conducted, the average cost of introducing new products has exceeded projections by a whopping 35 percent. When you consult Roy on this issue, he says, "If our working model passes the feasibility test, we use the model to determine production cost. At this point, we work closely with operational people to make sure all costs are covered. It's up to them and the bean counters in finance to come up with the right cost numbers. If they are wrong, it is not our fault. They own the problem." Since Roy, by his answer, indicates he is clearly not interested in taking responsibility for any problems, you conclude he has a Type Four personality.

Type Fours do not feel comfortable with the pressure that often comes with responsibility. Blaming others is one of their classic patterns. The best way to motivate Roy to help you with your product launch plans is to assure him that you will take full responsibility for any problems that develop. You can appeal to a Type Four's need for praise by assuring Roy that he will share in the celebration that will occur once the product successfully hits the market.

PERSUADING FOR ADVICE

There are many times you may think you know what you are doing and consequently don't need to seek out anyone's advice. Unfortunately, you may be choreographing your own failure. If you believe you have all the answers and refuse to solicit someone else's opinion, watch out. After your project has ended in disaster, you may find yourself asking, "Why didn't I talk to someone who knew more about this situation than I did?"

Part of the problem stems from the fact that it is often difficult to persuade a peer manager to take the time that's necessary to offer advice. Although seeking the advice of others does not always assure that the right decision will be made, it can dramatically improve your chances for making the right one.

The Situation

"You expect me to believe that the reason you want my advice is because we're supposed to act as a team?" Dan Bosley, manager of the marketing department, says in disbelief. His anger pushes the words out of his mouth, though he has stopped short of losing his temper.

You respond with, "Look Dan, what we're trying to accomplish here is important. It's how the company will succeed, and it's about the direction the CEO wants us to take." You know your frustration is showing, but how many times have you tried to get Dan's advice without any success? Your personality clashes with Dan have not helped the situation, but you desperately need his advice now on how to define a target market for one of the new services your organization is about to introduce.

Type Ones. If Dan is an insensitive and calculating Type One, he may consider you a rival who is competing against him for an upper management slot. In his mind, he has nothing to gain by helping you. You need to come up with something that you can trade for his advice. It could be a business favor such as agreeing to loan him one of your employees that he needs to complete a project or it could be as simple as a pair of hard-to-get football tickets.

Type Twos. If Dan becomes overtly emotional over your request for his advice, then something else is bothering him, which is typical of Type Twos. Type Twos often hold grudges for much longer than other types. You must have done something in the past that really irritated Dan. Find out what it was so that you can correct the situation and get him to provide the advice you need.

Type Threes. If Dan is a Type Three, he will jump at the opportunity to render his advice on anything when asked. Type Threes like to help others. In fact the problem is usually getting Type Threes not to give advice at the drop of a hat. Since Dan reacted the way he did, chances are that you approached him at the wrong time. He may have been in a depressed state of mind. Let him cool off for a day before approaching him again for advice.

Type Fours. Type Fours don't want to give out any advice for fear that they may be committing themselves to something that will require more work on their part. They'll avoid getting caught up in conversations that, in their opinion, could result in a commitment on their behalf. If you can assure Dan that all you want is his opinion and not his commitment, you stand a chance of getting him to talk to you.

PERSUADING FOR COOPERATION

Cooperation is one of the kindest words in the English language. In any effective long-term relationship, a sense of reciprocity must exist. If one team member is always the giver and the other always the taker, the first will feel he's being used by the second. The taker will feel that he got something for nothing. In this climate, cooperation is virtually impossible. To develop cooperative relationships, leaders must establish norms of reciprocity within the teams and among the players. People must believe that their goals are positively related so that as one moves toward obtaining her goal, the other person also moves toward obtaining his goal. Both parties understand that if one succeeds, the other succeeds. They realize that no one person can singlehandedly make a touchdown, teach a child, or build a quality car. A focus on a common purpose binds people together into a cooperative effort.

The Situation

You've done your best to prepare for your meeting with Elaine by gathering every piece of information she could possibly need. There is only one person in the company who can give you an outside chance of pulling this research project off and his name is Billy. Unfortunately, Billy doesn't work for you, he works for Elaine and you need to borrow him from her for six months. You're dreading this session with Elaine because she's hard enough to get along with even in the best of circumstances. The fact that you need one of her key employees to assist you in a project that she feels should have been assigned to her in the first place is not going to be something she wants to hear. When you walk into Elaine's office for your appointed meeting, there she is, sitting at her desk already tense and ready to strike out at you with all the venom of a cobra. How can you get her to cooperate with you?

Type Ones. Type One personalities usually have a loyalty to goals and a strong commitment to the organization they are working for. In your effort to motivate Elaine to loan you Billy, you might open your request like this: "As you know, Elaine, we are here this morning to discuss the company's performance in research and our desperate need to improve it. I need one of your employees to help me successfully complete our latest research project, which will set a precedent in this area and be of great help to the company. Can I count on you for your support?" By appealing to the loyalty that all Type Ones have, you should be able to get her support.

Type Twos. If you believe that Elaine has a Type Two personality, keep in mind that Type Twos are intensely loyal to people they trust. If they believe you, too, are loyal and sincere, they'll go out of their way to support you. Your approach to persuading Elaine to loan you Billy might start out with a statement that is designed to show your sincerity and gain her support. "Elaine, I am truly sorry that you did not get this assignment, but as we both know, that decision was made outside of our control. The fact is, I have the assignment and my chances of successfully completing the assignment are greatly reduced if I don't have the technical expertise that I need from one of your employees. Will you help me?"

Type Threes. Concentrate on minimizing the nervousness Type Threes have about anything that is new. Because of her inherent insecurities, Elaine is reluctant to loan you Billy because she doesn't believe the project will succeed. She's concerned that she, too, will be dragged down in its failure, if she's even remotely associated with it. The best way around this dilemma is to have Billy officially assigned to your team, reporting to you for the duration of the project. This action protects Elaine from any accusations of failure that could occur. On the other hand, if the project is a success, she stands to gain from some of the fanfare when you transfer Billy back to her team. You both win!

Type Fours. Type Fours are traditionally uncommitted individuals, and you are dealing with a peer manager who may have no special commitment to the company. Trying to motivate Elaine with helping the company probably won't work. A more viable approach might be to appeal to her desire to always be popular. Type Fours like to be popular. Suggest to her that by loaning you Billy, senior management will know that she has taken an active stand to support the successful completion of the project. Remind her of the executive celebration that will occur if the project is completed on time. Tell her she's invited!

PUTTING IT ALL TOGETHER

This chapter addressed techniques that you can employ to persuade your peers. A peer is an equal and in many cases, a rival. The different situations that were presented cast you into a range of scenarios from resolving hostile peer relationships to soliciting their support. You were introduced to several components that are essential to make the persuasion process work for you. We started with a discussion about communication, benefits, and justification. You use communications to sell your ideas and then justify your ideas with clear benefits that your peers can relate to. You learned how to use specific techniques when you need support or advice from peers. Your ability to effectively persuade peers is an essential component of your leadership credentials.

Influencing Attributes of the Personality Types

TYPE ONE	They are task-driven people who are influenced by people who can tell them exactly what needs to be done to complete an assignment.
TYPE TWO	They are sincere individuals who can be influenced by what people say they can do if they have confidence in them.
TYPE THREE	They will listen to everybody's ideas before they will allow themselves to be influenced to make a decision.
TYPE FOUR	They like to create lively interactions on issues as their way of determining who will influence their decision on an issue.

CHAPTER 12

Influencing Your Boss

You won't go anywhere if you don't know how to influence your boss.

THE EARLY GREEKS used three important words in their philosophy: ethos, pathos, and logos. These three words contain the essence of what you need to effectively influence your boss.

Ethos is your personal credibility, the faith your boss has in your integrity and competency. It's the trust that you inspire in your boss that motivates him or her to do good things for you like giving you a glowing performance review.

Pathos is the empathic side of the relationship between you and your boss. It assures that you have emotional trust. If he trusts you, he'll be willing to confide in you.

Logos is the logical part of the relationship. Your strategies, plans, and presentations must be logical and well thought out as far as your boss is concerned.

Most people will go straight to logos in an attempt to impress and motivate their boss. They'll try to convince the boss of the validity of their solution without first taking ethos and pathos into consideration. How many times have you heard the statement, "I had the only logical solution, but the boss didn't buy it. Instead, she chose that idiot's solution over mine." The idiot may not have had logos working for him, but you can rest assured he had mastered the ethos and pathos part of the relationship with his boss.

In this chapter I'll introduce you to different types of bosses and different techniques you can use to influence their thinking. We'll look at several tough subordinate/boss situations where the challenge will be to determine the personality types of the characters in our scenario. That will help you determine which technique (i.e., ethos, pathos, or logos) to use so that you can influence them to move in a direction that's favorable to you.

INFLUENCING BASICS

A leader's power to influence can range from finding just the right level of acceptance for the person she's trying to influence to knowing how to get the boss's buy-in to support her initiatives. Leaders who are adept at the art of influencing are also persuasive and engaging when they communicate to people. The art of influencing occurs at three levels. At its lowest level, people will follow a leader because they have to. The leader tells them to do something or suffer the consequences.

At the second level, people are influenced by a leader because of what she has done for them. They subsequently trust the leader who has exerted influence on them and will generally do whatever she asks. Morale rises, needs are met, and goals are realized.

At the third level of influence people follow a leader because of who she is and what she represents. The leader is known as a person of strong character and commitment. That's a given.

Challenge yourself to move to the third level where you successfully influence your boss because of who you are and what you represent. The discussions that follow will help you accomplish that objective, once you know the personality type of your boss. In addition to knowing which of the four personality types your boss belongs to, you must figure out his or her style of management or leadership. That, too, will influence how you attempt to project your influence.

DEALING WITH MICROMANAGERS

Micromanagers like to control everything in their domain and are capable of temporarily changing their personalities to throw their subordinates off guard. Although this is not easy to do, some are capable of showing all of the aggressive aspects of a Type One. However, they can quickly change into a loyal Type Two or adapt the relaxed behavior of a Type Three or Four if it suits their needs. If a micromanager finds himself in an adversarial relationship with an aggressive subordinate, he can lull the subordinate into complacency with all the known expertise of a Type Four.

Most micromanagers have predominately Type One or Two personalities. Both these personality types love detail.

The Situation

When your company formed its new Southeastern Region, the president's choice for general manager was Lynn Miller, a dynamic sales person in her late thirties. Lynn joined the company last year and rose rapidly into a middle-management position.

Her general manager appointment was controversial because it rocketed her past several more senior managers. In your first staff meeting with Lynn and her cadre of other subordinate managers, she tells everyone in no uncertain words exactly what she expects from her organization.

"You are all highly qualified for your jobs or you wouldn't be here. The object of this meeting is to tell you how I expect you to do your job and what I will require from each of you to control this division. Effective immediately, my signature must be on all expenses over $100. I also want to review and preapprove every project before it gets started. And, as a final note, monthly status reports will be replaced with weekly status reports. Are there any questions?" There are none, and as you walk out of the room, you think to yourself, "My God, I'm working for a micromanager. How will I be able to exert any influence over her?"

Type Ones. With rare exception, Type One micromanagers have no idea how they are viewed by their employees. This is in part because Type Ones are poor listeners, only hearing what they want to hear, and they insulate themselves from negative feedback. The key to influencing Lynn is to provide her with indirect feedback. For example, when the opportunity presents itself, instead of saying, "Lynn, you are a micromanager who is stifling creative thinking in our organization," try a more diplomatic and indirect approach. "Lynn, I am concerned that you don't have any confidence in my capabilities." When she responds with, "What do you mean?" seize the opportunity to show her how her micromanaging approach has led you to that conclusion.

If you address your concerns to Lynn in the proper manner, respecting her ego and not directly confronting her, she will trust you and give you wide freedom of action within your job.

Type Twos. Many micromanagers will have Type Two personalities. Remember, Type Twos love to analyze and over-analyze whatever task they take on. Lynn's requirement for detailed data from you on a recurring basis is the food she needs to support her analytical appetite. There is not much that you can do to change this personality attribute. Instead, you have to work around it.

The best way to stop Lynn from micromanaging you is to convince her that there are better ways to get her the information she wants. Suggest to her that what would really help her is a monthly status report submitted on a timely basis. Convince Lynn that your status report will contain everything she needs to know about the projects you're working on. She may want you to submit the report weekly, as opposed to monthly, which is still better than fielding her daily phone calls. If Lynn agrees with your status report alternative, make sure you include lots of detail in every report.

Type Threes. Type Three micromanagers tend to feel insecure about their jobs, which is the reason why they have become micromanagers. It's their way of making sure nothing slips by them that could get them in trouble later on down the line. At the same time, Type Threes are inherently lazy and don't like to wade through reams of detailed reports. The way to get Lynn off your back is to show her how you can make her job easier and give her the level of security she wants. Arrange to meet with her on a regular basis (e.g., once a week) to review the status of every project you're working on.

Type Fours. Type Four micromanagers believe they are helping you perform your job better. It is Lynn's way of showing you that she is a friend that you can trust. How do you convince her that you don't need her help and still preserve her trust in you? Discuss your desire to have more space with Lynn. Point out how important it is for you to feel you are running your own organization, with her help. of course. However, somewhere in the course of the conversation, make her aware that her micromanaging style bothers you a great deal. Type Fours are appreciative of people who will honestly share their feelings with them. Lynn should be willing to back off from her micromanagement style and give you more room.

INFLUENCING MACROMANAGERS

In contrast to micromanagers, macromanagers are only interested in the big picture. They want to know what's going on in the entire organization, and its aggregate output that's often measured by the bottom line. They have little interest in any of the details, a quality that often gets them into trouble.

The Situation

"I'm so furious I can't see straight," you say to your friend Alan. "I asked my boss, Greg, to review a couple of key accounting explanations that I want to put into our annual report. He tells me they're not important! When I ask him how he would know that since he hasn't seen my explanations, he tells me the only thing that counts is the bottom line, the company's gross profit. It's as if my job isn't important. No wonder he spends most of his time with the finance manager who always talks about the big picture. Somebody said Greg is a macromanager, but I think he's a macro idiot. What can make him come back down to earth?"

Type Ones. Type One macromanagers like to perceive themselves as power players. To them, macromanaging is the way to get to the top. Greg has very little interest in details and only wants to address the larger issues. One way you can influence Greg to appreciate your role is to wait for the right opportunity to convince him that the small picture details (i.e., numbers) can have a significant impact on the big picture. For example, suppose you discovered several accounting errors that significantly overstated the company's income. You bring it to Greg's attention before he is to go into an executive meeting to present the department's numbers. That should get him to appreciate the "total picture" of all the numbers that make up the annual report.

Type Twos. Type Two macromanagers like to talk about the big picture, but they have an appreciation for all of the micro processes, including the accounting functions that must be in place to make it all happen. Chances are that when Greg rebuffed your request to review your accounting explanations, he was preoccupied with some other more pressing matter. Approach Greg in a nonconfrontational manner and ask him why he isn't interested in reviewing the explanations with you. Listen carefully to what he has to say. He will probably apologize for his abrupt action and will be more motivated to listen to what you have to say about what should go into the annual report.

Type Threes. Type Threes think that independence is the key to getting to the top of the management chain. A few Type Threes will revert to macromanagement tactics as their perceived way of establishing their independence from the operations of the organization. This behavior provides Greg with the perfect excuse. By telling you he was focusing on the big picture, he is demonstrating his independence by not having to deal with you at the time. If you politely inform Greg that his reaction to your request for help upset you, it will probably not occur again. Cooperation within their organization is very important to Type Three macromanagers.

Type Fours. It is unlikely that a Type Four would be a macromanager since most of them are not independent thinkers. They like to work with everyone on everything. However, if Greg is a Type Four, you can rest assured that his rebuff of your request for his review of your annual report numbers had nothing to do with you personally. There was something else on his mind that distracted him from complying with your request. When you confront him for an explanation, you will get an unsolicited apology from him and a chance to show him your annual report numbers.

INFLUENCING BUREAUCRATS

Bureaucratic managers say they would like to accommodate you, but that rules and regulations prevent them from acting. Incapable of independent thought, bureaucrats are often found in the world of management. They thrive in old, established companies that are riddled with policies and procedures. Whenever bureaucrats feel threatened or endangered, they take refuge behind official directives, memoranda, or any other document that allows them to stop an action. Although there is nothing wrong with well-thought-out policies, bureaucrats go out of their way to interpret rules so that those rules support their point of view.

The Situation
It had been a great day for getting caught up at work. As the pleasant summer breeze drifts through the window in your office,

you decide to give your status report one more admiring review before you hit the send key to shoot it over to Ray Manning, that bureaucrat who is supposed to be your boss. At least he should be pleased when he finds out you have completed the design of the company's website three weeks ahead of schedule.

As you raise your finger to press the key, the ring of your phone interrupts you. It's Manning, who starts blurting out demands before you can even acknowledge that you are on the line. "It's about our website. I know you got approval to proceed with the project at the Critical Design Review meeting, but I don't want to take chances. Hold another meeting and ask for their approval again. Check with the Interstate Commerce Commission to see if we need anything else from them. Al Capp says he's got ideas that may improve the design you've come up with, so get with him and see what he's talking about. That's it for now. See ya!"

In a fit of rage, you bang the computer's delete key, sending your status report into the electronic graveyard. What can you do to influence this bureaucratic excuse for a boss who is driving you crazy?

Type Ones. Type One bureaucrats use their control of people and events to demonstrate how important they are. In our scenario, Ray actually thinks he is helping by insisting that duplicate steps be taken to assure the success of the company's website. Subconsciously, he's asserting his own status within the company, flexing his bureaucratic muscle to prove his importance. You have got to convince Ray that this project doesn't need the extra layer of steps he's just added. Try to get him to focus on the added cost the project will incur if you add the duplicate work that he is demanding. Show him how these expenses could be better deployed to support some other aspect of the organization.

Type Twos. Quality is of paramount importance to Type Two bureaucrats. Unfortunately, Ray has a misguided perception that duplicating activities on a project is the best way to assure that the highest standards will be met. If you challenge his approach, he will become suspicious that you are not interested in quality. You don't want that to happen. Assure Ray that quality control is of paramount importance in everything you do. Suggest to him that his dollars may be better spent monitoring the features of the website after it is up and running rather than duplicating checks that have already been performed.

Type Threes. Type Threes are often uninvolved in the work that gets done by their organization and will subsequently resort to implementing bureaucratic procedures as their mechanism to validate that what has been done has been done right. If Ray does not trust you, he will continue to raise bureaucratic barriers to the point where it will become almost impossible for you to complete any assignment. Type Three bureaucrats will begin removing bureaucratic barriers the moment they begin to trust you. Work on developing Ray's trust if you want to eliminate the bureaucratic obstacles that he is placing in your way. Show him you can complete assignments successfully and to his specifications.

Type Fours. Bureaucrats with Type Four personalities respond well to the "lesser of two evil" management ploys. Find a rule, regulation, or procedure that is at least as important as the one Ray is trying to force down your throat. Convince him that both his concerns and yours must be dealt with and that you are willing to do whatever has to be done to head off the potential problem. Bureaucrats often create more work for everyone, and since Type Fours do not like to work any more than they have to, leverage this attribute to convince Ray to modify his bureaucratic behavior.

INFLUENCING THE UNSCRUPULOUS

Unscrupulous managers are the con artists of the corporate world. What power mongers attempt to achieve with brute force, unscrupulous managers accomplish with finesse and lies. They promise employees everything and deliver nothing but tidbits of information and more promises. They like to give you company T-shirts, take you out to lunch, and send you one-line e-mail messages telling you how good you are—before they stab you in the back. A good con artist will put his arm around you, tell you how far you'll get by following his instructions, and then, pick your pocket and your brain. No matter how much he says he likes your work, if it suits his needs the con artist boss will tell his boss your mistakes are the cause of his problems.

The Situation

You worked harder than hard preparing this presentation for your boss, Jim Fowler. Three days ago he assigned you to present to the CEO the rationale behind her organization's expansion into the Southwest market. It's a real opportunity for you. If you impress the CEO and Jim with your knowledge of the market, you could possibly be rewarded with a promotion and an opportunity to transfer to Phoenix, the planned location for the regional office. At 10 A.M. sharp, you walk into Jim's office for your planned dry run of the presentation. For some reason, you find your coworker John sitting in a chair in front of Jim's desk.

Your surprised look catches Jim's attention, and when he tells you to sit down, you know that something is wrong. As soon as you are seated, he makes a statement that almost sends you to the floor: "After a considerable amount of thought, I have decided to have John make the presentation rather than you. This should not be considered as a negative reflection on you. I just think that John has a more in-depth knowledge of what's going on in the market than you do. Do you have any problem with my decision?"

You manage to blurt out a "No," and when Jim invites you to stick around while John makes a practice presentation from your charts, you ask if you can be excused. As you quickly exit Jim's office, you mutter to yourself, "This is the second time that two-faced con artist has pulled a stunt like this on me, and I am not going to take it any more."

Type Ones. One of the inherent weaknesses of Type One bosses is that they can be very insensitive to the feelings of their employees. When insensitivity is combined with the conniving attributes of a con artist, you have all of the makings for a difficult situation. If you are up to it, confront Jim and call his attention to how he has treated you. Ask him why he chose John over you to make the presentation. If you are not satisfied with his answer, grin and bear it until you can either transfer out of his organization, find another job outside the company, or wait until Jim moves into another position. Remember that Type Ones don't mind direct confrontation, as long as you're straightforward with them.

Type Twos. Con-artist behavior is contrary to normal Type Two personalities, who are typically loyal to their employees. Before you approach Jim on this issue, first determine if he trusts you. If you are new on the job, he may not have had time to develop confidence in your capabilities. If this is the case, then he may not have had any other recourse but to call on John to make the presentation until he gets the opportunity to know you better. If you approach Jim with a positive attitude, he should be willing to give you an honest answer to your question: "Do you have confidence in my capabilities?" Listen carefully to his answer. If you conclude that Jim is in fact a first-rate con artist, you may have no other choice but to leave his organization.

Type Threes. Type Threes can demonstrate dishonest attributes that complement their con-artist behavior. If you believe that Jim is dishonest and deceitful, there is nothing that you can do to influence him to change. You may talk to him about your dilemma, and he will give you all of the appearances that he understands and wants to cooperate with you. Watch out because you're being conned again and if he feels threatened by the possibility that you might expose him by talking behind his back, he will find a way to fire you. Your best option is to find another boss that you can trust.

Type Fours. You will seldom find a con-artist boss with a Type Four personality. It's not inherent in their friendly nature, but if Jim is a Type Four and he displays con-artist traits, watch out. He'll come across as the friendliest, most trusting boss you have ever had. If Jim is good at covering his deceitful nature, you may find yourself apologizing to him when he pulls the presentation assignment out from under you. Be careful not to let that happen. If you threaten to escalate his con-artist behavior to his boss, he'll back off for fear of exposure. He'll also never give you a promotion and will find a way to get you out of his organization, so start looking for another job.

ARROGANT BOSSES

Any manager is capable of being arrogant on occasion, but the real jerks make arrogance a way of life. They don't have the guts to admit to their arrogance and have a difficult time managing their own career or any assignment given to them, let alone helping employees progress on their own career path. Unfortunately, in spite of their arrogance, they do occasionally creep into upper management; either they know somebody on the inside or another arrogant executive thinks it would be nice to have company in the management ranks.

Arrogant managers reduce the effectiveness of anybody who works for them. They are good at blocking initiatives and thwarting ambition. In extreme cases, arrogant managers can threaten their subordinates to the point where the employees are unwilling to take any risks. It's hard to say how many arrogant bosses there really are, in part because of the subjectivity of the definition. However, one only has to ask trusted colleagues, "Have you ever worked for an arrogant boss?" to get a feeling for how widespread the problem is. Almost everybody has or will work for an arrogant boss at least once during their career.

The Situation

A person's arrogance quickly reveals itself when she perpetually makes critical comments about others. Perhaps she resents their success or is jealous of their achievements. One of the most noticeable attributes of an arrogant boss is the way she reacts to criticism. She can't stand it if she believes the laughter or criticism is being directed at her. Often she'll react in a manner that is completely out of proportion to the act.

You're really upset! You've just completed another trying session with your boss, Helen Redding, that unadulterated jerk whose brains are always on vacation. This world-class bozo has taken every good idea that you've had and thrown it back into your face with words like, "Are you out of your mind?" Once, she even suggested that you see the company psychologist. Your raise for next year has already been denied and when you requested a transfer, she tells you there is no way she would risk her reputation on transferring a "questionable employee" to another department. It's clear to you that she wants you to voluntarily resign, but you vow not to accommodate her.

Type Ones. If you are working for a hard-core Type One arrogant boss who wants everything done her own way, you have a serious problem. You're probably tired of being pushed around, fed up with not being allowed to do what is right, and watching helplessly at the lack of progress you're making in your career. To make matters worse, Helen has been with the company forever and her boss, who is also arrogant, supports her. So much for the thought that if you hang in there, you'll outlast her! What are your options? You could get another job in the same company assuming that Helen will allow you to transfer. In order to facilitate this, be prepared to bite your lip and play up to her ego. Tell Helen whatever you believe she wants to hear and do whatever she asks you to do. Make her think you are her loyal and most trusted employee. Then, ask her to sign your transfer request.

Type Twos. As much as you may think that your boss is a miserable worm, evaluate where you may fit into Helen's professional life. Perhaps her attitude toward you would change abruptly if you did something to make her happy. Type Twos want their feelings to be understood and they'll support anybody whom understands that concept. If Helen believes that you are not committed to her, she will make your life miserable and may eventually terminate you. As long as she believes you support her and are helping meet her goals, she will reward your good performance with, hopefully, a transfer.

Type Threes. When Helen is in a good mood, suggest to her that you need her help. The need for help appeals to the ego of Type Threes so you'll be on track to win her favor and support. When she asks you what kind of help you need, tell her you love working for her, but you're getting bored with your current position. Ask her if she will assist you in transferring to another department where they have just opened up a position that is of interest to you. If she agrees to help you with your transfer request, you're on your way out of a bad situation. If Helen rejects your request, update your resume and find a job in another organization.

Type Fours. Arrogant managers with Type Four personalities would normally be relatively easy to influence if they were total idiots, but they are not. Most Type Fours are intelligent people who are sometimes blessed with obnoxious behavior. Keep in mind that they are trusting individuals who want you to always be truthful with them. Since it would not be prudent to tell Helen that she's arrogant, start by telling her what she wants to hear (i.e., how competent she is). As you gain her confidence, encourage her to allow you to have your own way. Make yourself absolutely indispensable to her organization. In the process, Helen will think of you as being more useful whenever she asks for your help. Continue playing the role to the point where she believes that you are indispensable and believes she couldn't meet her goals without your support. Since most Type Fours dislike doing work that isn't fun, consider gaining Helen's trust by offering to take a burdensome assignment off her hands. Once you've accomplished this, you are ready to have a healthy conversation with Helen to solicit her help in transferring you to another organization.

INFLUENCING POWER ADDICTS

Power-addict managers feed off power. The more they can get, the more they want. They're single-minded, egomaniacal individuals who are only interested in their own personal empires. Driven to control everything and everyone in sight, they must have the last word and be the final authority on any subject, no matter how minor. They are more interested in bossing people around than they are in getting anything done. If you stand in their way, they will use all of their energies to get rid of you, even if you are right and they are wrong.

The Situation

When you first met your boss, Bill Beagles, it was obvious that he had mixed feelings about you. Over a short time, it became obvious that the man did not like you personally or professionally for reasons beyond your comprehension. You have always gone out of your way to be polite, accepted every assignment he has given you with enthusiasm, and always completed your projects on time. Your relationship with Bill has deteriorated to the point where he refuses to meet with you to discuss anything. When you call to ask if he could meet with you to discuss your status report, Bill replies, "Yeah, but I have no time for you right now. You are not one of my top priorities so I will have to get back to you on a meeting time." He, of course, will never get back to you. It has become apparent to you that the man is a power addict and that you are nothing more than a pawn in Bill's chess game.

Type Ones. Type One power addicts have no use for anybody that gets in their way. They savor confrontations more than arbitration. Acquiring power over people is more important to them than merely having power. They want the pleasure of transforming someone who is assertive to someone who squirms at their presence. The way to influence a Type One power addict boss is to selectively challenge his authority to exercise power over you. On a daily basis, play up to Bill's ego by telling him what he wants to hear, letting him think he's in charge. Over time, you may be able to manipulate him to do whatever you want him to do.

Type Twos. Type Two power addicts love to exercise control and want you to act as though you couldn't get anything done without their help. To survive, be willing to continually bow to Bill's authority by telling him how much you value his help and constantly praise his ideas. You have to get Bill to trust you, which is very important to Type Twos. Over time, he may allow you to "take charge" of whatever assignment he gives you and will leave you alone. If that doesn't happen, it will at least buy you the time you need to find another job.

Type Threes. Type Three power addicts want to at least pretend to be understanding in a situation. If you tell Bill that you agree with his power-oriented decisions, you may be able to throw him off guard. However, let him know that he wouldn't be making power-oriented decisions if he was aware of what he was doing to the organization. When he asks you what you mean, be prepared to explain to him how his management style is stifling the productivity of the department. Tell him that you know how to fix the situation and give it your best shot. If it works, great! Otherwise, find another job.

Type Fours. Type Four power addicts are very insensitive managers. To them, you are nothing more than a pawn in a chess game that they can use to get whatever they want with a minimum amount of work on their part. If you approach Bill with an idea, be prepared to answer his hidden question: "What's in it for me?" Tell Bill what he wants to hear and you will eventually earn his trust. Unless he's paranoid, he will leave you alone most of the time to do what you want to do as long as he believes that whatever you are doing will ultimately benefit him.

INFLUENCING CHAMELEONS

In the classic movie *The Best Little Whorehouse in Texas,* the governor of Texas closely follows the polls to measure the public's opinion of him and dances around the mood of the electorate, singing, "Now you see me, now you don't!" He is a perfect human chameleon, agreeing with one opinion one day and switching to another the next day. You never know what a chameleon is going to do until she actually does it. Experts at sleight-of-mouth techniques, chameleon managers cannot be trusted. They are manipulative and extremely deceptive.

The Situation

The attitude of your hyper-masculine boss, Sam, reminds you of a college football coach, his position before joining the company. "No woman is going to be hired as a sales rep in this organization as long as I'm in charge." If only he had stayed where he was, coaching a team that seldom won a game. Unfortunately, he is smart enough to know that his outdated attitude could get him into some serious trouble with the affirmative-action people. Whenever the question comes up as to why his entire sales force is male, he always uses his carefully rehearsed answer: "We've been discussing it. Had a meeting on the subject just the other day. I don't know what's causing the problem, but you can rest assured I'm going to get at the bottom of this thing soon!"

Like a chameleon, Sam can change his colors quicker than any executive you have ever seen. You have just interviewed an outstanding female candidate to take over one of your sales regions that desperately needs help. Your spineless personnel manager asks you to get Sam to sign the new-hire paperwork before he will do anything with the requisition. How do you influence Sam to accept the first female on your sales team?

Type Ones. Calculating Type One bosses are fully cognizant of the affirmative-action laws and regulations. Do not mention the topic to Sam when you give him the requisition to sign. In his true chameleon fashion, he will tell you to leave it on his desk so that he can review it later. Pin him down. Be direct with him. He can relate to that. Tell him that you will bring the requisition back to him at a specific time for his signature. If he insists that you leave the document with him, ask him when you can pick it up.

Type Twos. Type Two chameleons tend to be unrealistic individuals who, for whatever reason, believe they can forestall the inevitable forever. If you remind Sam of the key affirmative-action points of law, emphasizing the personal liability side of the law, you'll quickly get his attention and he'll sign the requisition.

Type Threes. Type Threes are reluctant and unsure people who can develop the color-changing attributes of chameleons to hide from the inevitable. Use the same legal awareness tactics that you would use for Type Twos to motivate a Type Three to sign your requisition. If Sam still refuses to sign, tell him you will turn the matter over to the Human Resource Department. He'll sign.

Type Fours. To a Type Four, the role of a chameleon is nothing more than one of the many games that he enjoys playing. Take the fun out of the game by informing him of the legal consequences of his actions. He will quickly stop playing the game and sign your requisition.

INFLUENCING LONE RANGERS

Managers who are lone rangers want to be left alone to do things on their own and at their own pace. If they had their choice, they would prefer to work by themselves in a desolate mountain cabin. They exhibit little concern about the people who work for them. As a result, they drive away talent from their organizations. Talented employees won't work for somebody who can't or won't give them something back for their efforts.

If you work for a lone ranger, find out what he likes and doesn't like to do. Volunteer to take on any administrative tasks or other work that he may hate, such as interacting with people. If he knows you're willing to handle all of his interpersonal matters, he will support you in achieving your leadership objectives.

The Situation

If your boss shared even the slightest hint of an opinion with you, you would be relieved. His uncanny ability to sit for hours in his office and stare into space is unnerving to say the least. Looking into his eyes is like gazing into a vacant house. Once again, you repeat your question to see if you can get an answer: "Marcia

Miller has an opening in her organization and I would like to apply for the job. Is that all right with you, Gary?" After what seems an eternity, you finally get a response: "I don't know . . . Leave me alone for awhile so I can think about it!" At least you managed to get a response out of the lone ranger, but you're concerned that if you leave him alone, you'll never get an answer.

Type Ones. If you are attempting to influence a Type One lone ranger boss who has a difficult time communicating with you or anybody else for that matter, take the initiative and communicate with him. To spare Gary the burden of interacting with you, write him a memo. Don't ask for his permission; just tell him what you plan to do and ask for his comments, pointing out how he can help you. Your memo should not have a pleading tone. It should be very businesslike and to the point. When Gary reads your memo, it may force him to talk to you or, at the very least, write you a response.

Type Twos. If Gary has a Type Two personality, there is something that is bothering your lone ranger boss that goes beyond anything you have done, so don't take the situation personally. There's a good chance that he is facing personal problems that are causing him to lose his focus on anything you may have requested from him. If you can, give him a couple of days to recover from whatever is bothering him, and approach him again for an answer to your question.

Type Threes. Type Three lone rangers tend to be uncommitted when asked to make basic management decisions. If you are dealing with one who is uncomfortable dealing with people in the first place, you may never get him to give you a direct answer to your transfer request. If, after several attempts, you are unsuccessful at getting Gary to give you the commitment that you want, simply tell him you will escalate your request to his boss. The threat of this will get his immediate attention. Type Threes do not like to be threatened.

Type Fours. Type Fours are not normally quiet, antisocial individuals. If Gary is a Type Four, it is possible that he is demonstrating this behavior to be obnoxious. In this particular situation, it is appropriate to let Gary know how serious you are about getting an answer to your transfer request. Tell him that if he cannot give you an answer to your question within a reasonable period of time, you will take the matter up with his boss. Type Fours will do anything to avoid confrontations. Gary will quickly accommodate your request.

INFLUENCING FIREFIGHTERS

Managers who consider themselves firefighters thrive on a crisis environment. They are never content to have things under control and are always on the lookout for a new catastrophe, a new fire to extinguish. If none exist, they will find an assortment of insignificant issues and blow each of them up to colossal proportions so that they can marshal their forces to prevent whatever fire they predict will break out if no action is taken. Firefighters have no sense of business politics and do not know how to set priorities. As a result, they are very demanding on their people and expect them to be as driven as they are by crisis situations. Firefighters drive the people who work for them crazy by constantly changing their priorities and creating new fires. Firefighter managers are disasters at administrating or planning anything. They'll stop at nothing to meet a crisis objective, and because they do everything in extremes, if they make a mistake, it can be a whopper!

The Situation

Valerie Haskell comes rushing into your office and slams the door. "You won't believe what I just discovered, and you have got to promise me you won't breathe a word to anybody about what I am about to tell you." She waits for your response as you think, "God, this woman loves crisis, but she's the boss so what am I going to do? I'll just have to stay with her organization until something better comes along."

When you tell her your lips are sealed, she continues. As it turns out, the crisis that Valerie has discovered is, in your mind, an opportunity for you. One of the company's major competitors has just declared bankruptcy in Seattle, which opens up the entire northwest market region to your company. Valerie believes there is nobody within the organization who is capable of taking over this newfound opportunity. In the true spirit of a firefighter, she has created a crisis before she has even started looking for a qualified person. Maybe you're the one, and she doesn't know it yet!

Type Ones and Twos. Firefighter managers who have Type One or Two personalities are often uncomfortable when they have nothing Important To Do. They've got to be going somewhere or meeting someone all the time to sate their need for excitement. If left alone, you will find them staring out a window looking for the next fire. Type Ones and Twos typically know how to set goals and have an appreciation for the importance goals play in achieving long-term objectives. Valerie has created a crisis out of the need to find someone to manage the new northwest region. The direct way to influence her is to offer her a solution to the problem; one that extinguishes the fire in her mind. Your interest in taking over the northwest region may be just what the doctor ordered.

Type Threes and Fours. Firefighter managers who have Type Three or Four personalities often do not have a concrete set of goals that they're striving to meet. If your boss is a Type Three firefighter, goals are moderately important and she will often create a crisis situation that forces her to establish a goal. Valerie has created a situation (the northwest region) that demands a goal (to find a regional manager). The best way to influence her is to create the goal and the steps she needs to go through to meet that goal. Offer yourself up as the new Northwest Regional Manager. The same approach will work with a Type Four manager. They are optimistic individuals, so stress the fact that you are performer who likes to avoid conflicts with your staff.

PUTTING IT ALL TOGETHER

Influence is the act of producing an effect on someone without exerting force or command. Influence can be used for personal gain, as was demonstrated in this chapter. You were shown several examples of how it can be used to affect your boss in indirect or intangible ways. Your ability to influence your boss begins with finding just the right words to build agreement from them to support your initiatives. The words that you use must be both persuasive and engaging to capture their attention.

We looked at several different types of bosses and how the four personality types manifest themselves in those boss types. We examined how to use different techniques to influence their thinking. Several tough subordinate/boss situations were created where you were challenged to determine the personality types of the characters in the situation scenarios. These exercises were designed to help you devise techniques to influence your boss to help you move in a direction that's favorable to you.

Inspiring Attributes of the Personality Types

TYPE ONE	They have powerful personalities who are inspired by people who can tell them exactly what needs to be done to move ahead.
TYPE TWO	They are deliberate and sincere individuals who are inspired by what people say they can do if they believe they really can do it.
TYPE THREE	They have gentle personalities and will listen to everyone's inspiring idea before they will select the one they like.
TYPE FOUR	They are optimistic individuals who are inspired by people they trust and who support issues that are important to them.

CHAPTER 13

Inspiring Upper Management

Leaders who inspire create resonance and move people with their compelling vision.

INSPIRING IS ONE of the most exciting action verbs in the English language. It means to influence, to move, or to guide. Executives are inspired by people who are enthusiastic, energetic, and positive about the future. If you want to be a leader who is successful at inspiring upper management, you must be able to communicate your vision in a way that encourages them to endorse you.

Back in 2000, nobody knew who Suze Orman was other than the few people who used her as their stockbroker. What limited success she had achieved was the consequence of her ability to talk. But Orman did more than just talk. She inspired people who listened to her thoughts on personal finance. Her ability to inspire served her well as her career moved onto the fast track when she was invited to appear on the Oprah Winfrey show.

Suze Orman's ability to inspire people has rewarded her with remarkable success and incredible international influence. She is one of the highest-paid talk show hosts in the country, broadcasting her television show to millions of people in the United States alone. As one of the greatest proactive leaders ever, she has never lost sight of her lifelong goal to inspire everyone she touches.

Good proactive leaders are constantly monitoring the dynamic changes that are occurring in their business environments from keeping track of consumer buying patterns to evaluating the strategic maneuvers of their competitors. They listen carefully to what people tell them and respond accordingly with an inspirational drive that enables them to get whatever job upper management wants done. Their enthusiasm, energy, and positive attitude make their objectives more meaningful. In this chapter, we show you how to use inspirational techniques on upper management to help move your leadership career onto the fast track. In the process, you will learn how to quickly recognize the often "difficult-to-read" personality types of upper-level managers so that you can adjust your inspirational tactics accordingly.

INSPIRING IMPRESSIONS

Impressions begin with what others see in you. They become inspiring impressions when they make people get excited about what they see and hear. In a business climate, presentations offer you an opportunity to create a good first impression. If you are standing in front of a group of executives about to make a presentation, it is absolutely critical that the first one minute of your presentation comes across as positive rather than negative. In his book *Presentations Plus,* David Peoples contends that 75 percent of what people know comes to them visually and 25 percent comes to them from what they hear. Since human beings are visually orientated, presentations that include a positive visual impression of yourself and your presentation material can create impressions that are more important than the words you use. Information that is seen has a much greater chance of being remembered than information that is heard.

The more you know about the culture and personality types of each executive in the group, the more accurately you can predict their expectations and tailor your presentation to create a favorable impression. While it is highly unlikely all the executives in a group presentation will have the same personality type, typing their personalities in advance of the meeting to gauge how you should structure your presentation is absolutely critical to your success.

Being a skillful presenter takes a lot of preparation, practice, and communication skills. Do you have these skills? Review the following list and put a check mark next to the ones you feel you need to work on. While no one will meet all of the quality points listed, a successful presenter will make a continuous effort to improve upon their presentation skills. Here are several ideas for you to consider:

Grab their attention. Good presenters accept the fact that they are, to some degree, entertainers. They exude high-energy enthusiasm for the topic they are discussing in a way that excites their audience. To grab the attention of a group of executives at the outset of your presentation, show them the big picture. If applicable, use a white board to go over key project status points. For example, you may want to compare projected costs to actual costs, noting the reasons for any over- or underruns.

Be informed. It's not only important for you to know your presentation material, you must also be perceived by the audience as being knowledgeable about the subject you're addressing.

Always know where you're going in your presentation. Sense how your presentation is being perceived by your audience, and change course if you sense unrest.

Be consistent. The more consistent you are in all your methods of communication, the more favorable will be your first impression. Consistency in communication includes body language, voice, and words. If you're presenting important figures and smiling at the same time, you are not consistent in emphasizing the importance of the message you're trying to convey. A more serious look might be in order for this part of your presentation.

Expect the unexpected. Skillful leaders always control their presentations, regardless of internal or external disruptions. Always have a backup plan to cover the unexpected. For example, if the overhead projector goes out, have manual charts available.

Engage your audience. Smiling and head nodding are the most powerful nonverbal clues you can use when speaking. Start off your presentation with direct eye contact and adjust from there. Most presentations are designed to get an audience to think or act in a specific way. Good leaders are persuasive throughout their presentation. Depending upon the setting, they welcome questions from their audiences. Be quick on your feet, and give precise and meaningful answers to any questions. If you're dealing with an unpopular or controversial subject, step up to the table and share your honest opinions with the audience. Never make cramped gestures or extraneous movements or fiddle with objects. That can distract the audience from your presentation.

Concentrate on delivery. Delivering an interesting, powerful presentation requires more than just being an expert in the subject and reciting what you have rehearsed. What do you sound like when you make a presentation (i.e., inspirational, enthusiastic, etc.)? Your voice tells a lot about your personality, attitude, and level of confidence. Does what you say capture your audience's attention? Communicate your message in a clear and concise manner that the audience can understand.

INSPIRING ENCOUNTERS

It goes without saying that you can't inspire someone until you encounter him either on a formal or informal basis. An executive may approach you and ask you a question on a subject he thinks you know something about. Executive encounters offer you an opportunity to demonstrate how well versed you are in a topic that's of interest to someone who could influence your career. However, even if you are the world's foremost expert on that subject, if you are not able to present the desired information in a format that inspires and engages your listener, you will not accumulate any career points. In fact, you could even lose points. You want to make all of your encounters with upper management inspiring encounters. Here are three issues to keep in mind when you're involved in such encounters:

1. **First impression.** The first thirty-second impression an executive develops about you will be based on your facial expressions, physical movements, and the tone of your voice. If that picture is positive, you will make an immediate and favorable impression. If the impression is negative, your odds are significantly reduced and you probably won't get a second chance. If an executive tells you politely

that she will digest what you have said and will get back with you later, you can rest assured that you have not made a favorable first impression.

2. **Appearance.** Your appearance is an important factor in executive encounters. Personal appearance can influence a manager's perception of you and may even determine his attitude toward you after your encounter. People whose appearance suggests professionalism are treated measurably better than those whose appearances suggest sloppy or careless demeanor. Like it or not, most executives think of themselves as professionals, and they look for the same thing in those they encounter.

3. **Language.** The executives you encounter must believe that you are a person who is committed to the organization and loyal to the cause. Only when they believe that will they take your comments seriously. They'll examine your nonverbal communication from facial expressions to body movements to judge your initial worth and the value of the information you give. Language is one of the most revealing differences between committed people and those with little commitment. You want to come across as a committed person in everything you say.

STRATEGIC ENCOUNTERS

Arranging strategic meetings with key senior managers is one of the most powerful political tools you have in your "get ahead" leadership arsenal. Let's say you have a brilliant idea for a new product that when developed and introduced into the market could catapult your company into *Fortune* 500 heaven. You know you're the best person to successfully carry off your idea, and there is only one executive who can give you the authority to proceed.

How do you meet with this person and inspire him to move on your idea? You initiate a strategic encounter.

The Situation

You're at the company's TGIF party to celebrate the closure of its record high earnings fiscal year. It presents a perfect opportunity for you to rub elbows with Haley Williams, the division's new president. You've heard through a reliable grapevine that she has already started to scout for a senior vice president of marketing. Why not see if you can get a chance to step up to the plate and hit a home run? To take advantage of the situation, you walk up to Haley, introduce yourself, and start a casual conversation with her. You tell yourself, "When the timing is right, I will introduce her to my new product idea." Then you wonder, "When will I know when the timing is right?"

If the conversation is going well, it is the right time. You might simply say, "Haley, I have an exciting new product idea that I would like to tell you about. Could I stop by your office tomorrow and show you what I'm talking about?" When she agrees, you have accomplished your primary mission. Continue on with your casual conversation. You'll have the rest of the night to prepare for tomorrow's presentation. As you drive to work the next morning, you wonder what you're going to say at your one-on-one meeting with Haley. You've created an outstanding presentation complete with illustrative examples that will show this executive that you clearly know what you are doing. Will it cater to her personality type?

Type Ones. Let's assume that Haley has a Type One personality. Typically, these are the most difficult of all the personalities to inspire. They have limited attention spans and about as much patience as a piranha that is about to attack a floating piece of meat in the Amazon River. Begin your presentation by showing a rich lode of data with meaningful charts that addresses exactly what Haley wants to know. That should solidify your initial position. If you fail to make a favorable first impression with a Type One executive, you probably won't get a second chance. If Haley tells you politely that she will digest what you have said and will get back with you later, you can rest assured that you have not made a favorable impression on her. Your chances of getting on the fast track with the support of this particular executive are slim to none.

Type Twos. If Haley has a Type Two personality, it will take her about thirty seconds to form an impression of you based upon your general appearance and the tone of your voice. If that picture is positive, you have a chance to make a favorable impression on her. If her impression is negative, your odds of inspiring her to accept your ideas are significantly reduced. More than anything, your appearance influences Type Two's perception of you and may even determine her attitude toward you at the outset of a meeting. That's why people whose appearance suggests high status are treated measurably better than those whose appearance suggests low status. It is a fact of life that most Type Two executives think of themselves as being of high status.

Type Threes. If Haley is a Type Three executive, nonverbal communications from appearance to facial expression to movement is the primary ingredient she will use to judge your initial presentation. She'll rely on it even more heavily if the words in your presentation give a contradictory message. She must believe that you are a person who is committed to the company and loyal to the causes of the organization first before she will endorse anything you are asking for. Type Threes are patient individuals and will often give you a second chance to recover from an initial bad presentation. Don't count on a third chance.

Type Fours. Facial expressions are extremely important to Type Four executives. What might your face say to Haley at your first meeting? If you demonstrate frustration with a perpetual frown on your forehead or show a blank expression on your face, you are showing her you're not interested. You're showing her you are nervous and anxious if you have a tight smile. Always keep in mind that a real smile is the most important facial expression you have for communicating. It is your chief component for attracting attention and radiates a level of confidence that Type Four executives are looking for. Also, pay attention to how you sound when you talk. Your voice tells a lot about your personality, attitude, and level of confidence. Communicate your message in a clear and concise manner that Type Four executives will appreciate.

SUDDEN ENCOUNTERS

Top-flight executives in every business profession all share one key capability. They know how to present themselves, their ideas, and get their point across in a brief period of time. It's always a pleasure to watch a good executive speaker and listen to his perfect choice of words and his controlled tone of voice. He displays an easy and commanding stance, and uses sophisticated body language, such as turning to face everyone, showing that every member of the audience is important to him. If you have the opportunity to make a presentation to a group of executives, you, too, can, in a relatively short period of time, make a lasting impression on them. Who will they be thinking about when the next promotional opportunity comes up?

The Situation

As you walk down the hallway past the boardroom, you're startled when the door swings open and your boss, Jerry Madden, suddenly appears in front of you. "Quick, get in here and tell the board of directors everything you know about the Peabody project. They think we're out of control, and my backside is on the line if you don't convince them otherwise." Before you can utter a response, Jerry grabs you by the arm, and you're suddenly standing at the head of the conference table facing a crowd of twelve angry board members.

As Jerry introduces you to the board, you quickly survey the group to determine how you will structure this ad-hoc presentation. If you believe that most of the audience is made up of Type Ones and Twos, then you'll start your presentation off with a quantifiable approach that appeals to them. Next, appeal to the optimistic needs of the Type Threes who are in the meeting. If the ranking executive in the group happens to have a Type Four personality, use exciting words to tell your story. You conclude your thirty-second personality type survey as you simultaneously introduce yourself. As near as you can tell, all four personality types are represented.

Type Ones. To grab the attention of the Type One board members, show them the big picture of the project at the very outset of your presentation. Since you haven't had time to prepare any briefing charts, make use of the white board to quickly recap key project status points. For example, you may want to show them key task start and completion dates, noting the reasons for any missed schedules and what the recovery plan is.

Type Twos. Remember, the more consistent you can make what you say, the more favorable an impression you'll make on the Type Two board members. Consistency covers all three channels of communications that you will be using (i.e., body language, voice, and words). If you are presenting some serious numbers on the white board and smiling at the same time, you're not consistent in the message you're trying to convey. A more serious look is in order. Always know what your face is saying. It is your most controllable nonverbal clue and the one that Type Two executives will be relying on to gauge your attitude.

Type Threes. Gesture with purpose, and always look directly at your Type Three executives. Don't make cramped gestures like fiddling with coins, bracelets, pens, ties, or other objects, which will distract the Type Three board members. If you look and act like you are in control of the situation, they will be comfortable. Type Threes are team players, so let them know that the Peabody project is a team effort.

Type Fours. Smiling and head nodding are the most powerful nonverbal clues you can use when addressing Type Fours. Start your presentation off with direct eye contact with them. If you are uncomfortable about making eye contact, look at the person's forehead. Unless they are very close to you, they will not be able to tell if you are avoiding direct eye contact. Type Fours like colorful, artistic graphs and charts instead of bland tables and charts. Since you haven't had time to prepare any artistic charts, use colored felt pens when you draw illustrations on the white board.

SOCIAL ENCOUNTERS

The pen is mightier than the sword, but neither is mightier than the mouth, especially when it comes to creating impressions with executives whom you encounter in social settings. Voice communication is second only to body language as a means of communicating in such settings. In face-to-face interactions, it isn't enough to be physically attractive. The moment you open your mouth, you either confirm or deny the initial impression that a person has about you. If you sound harsh and abrasive, you probably will be viewed the same way. If you sound timid and insecure, you will be considered as such.

Mark Twain once said, "Better to keep your mouth shut and be thought a fool than to open it and remove all doubt."

The Situation

The annual Chamber of Commerce Christmas party is an event you've been coming to for years. It offers you a great opportunity to rub elbows with the community's business leaders and have a great time in the process. As you glance over at the bar, there's Ed Rickels, the senior vice president of your company, sitting by himself. Boy, would you like to get to know him a little better. Word has it that he's about to become the new CEO when Harrison retires next month. As you walk over to where Ed is sitting, you size up his personality type as you carefully consider what you're going to say.

Type Ones. When you walk up to Ed and introduce yourself, he abruptly asks you, "What do you want?" You're not surprised because you guessed that he was a Type One who likes to intimidate people. The best way to stop him from intimidating you is to be deferential and polite, "Oh, I'm sorry if I bothered you. I just wanted to introduce myself and chat with you for a moment." He'll quickly end his abrupt behavior and will allow you to enter into a healthy social conversation with him, which hopefully will give you a chance to get to know him better.

Type Twos. When you walk up to Ed and introduce yourself, you note that he at first has a suspicious look in his eye, as if he's wondering what you are after. This is a Type Two characteristic. To neutralize the situation, avoid getting into any discussion about company business. Talk about subjects of mutual interest like sports or the upcoming seasonal activities before you enter into more serious subjects. Ask probing questions to find a subject that is of interest to him. "Ed, what is your favorite sport?"

Type Threes. When you begin your conversation with Ed, you can't help but think that he is one of the most unenthusiastic people you've ever talked to. Type Threes can be unenthusiastic unless you can discover a subject that is of interest to them. Ask Ed what he likes to do when he's not working, and then talk about it to spark his enthusiasm. If he likes to do something that you know nothing about, you might simply say, "Ed, that really sounds interesting. Tell me about it." Get him to do the talking about a subject that he's comfortable with.

Type Fours. Type Fours like to be in settings that are calm and controlled where there is no tension or anxiety. Ed's first priority is to relax and enjoy the party setting. His last wish is to get trapped into a conversation about some work-related subject. When you address Type Fours, keep your conversation light and friendly. Avoid talking about anything concerning work and address subjects that you know are of interest to him such as golf, tennis, barbecuing, or whatever.

FAST-TRACK ENCOUNTERS

The expression "fast track" has different connotations in different organizations. But when you get rid of all the hype associated with the term, it means individuals management has chosen to put on the fast track get significant promotions if they meet their assigned company goals. The specific objectives of the goal are usually well defined, the tasks that must be completed are already identified, and most important, a completion date has been established. The only missing component is a person the company executives trust to head up the effort to make it happen. In the scenario that follows, you have an opportunity to lead a fast-track team that has been assigned to open a major new market for the company. You have been asked to make a presentation to a selection committee made up of four company executives. Your presentation must show them why you are the right person for this fast-track assignment.

The Situation

As the four executives enter the small conference room and take their places around the table, Latin music is playing softly in the background. Notebooks containing information packets have been placed on the meeting table in front of each chair. Fortunately, or unfortunately, you are blessed with four executives, each with a different personality. Because your Type One and

Two executives won't care what kind of paper you used in the notebook, you chose a good quality stock with a rough linen-like texture that you know will appeal to the Type Three and Four executives. You have carefully planned this presentation to inspire each personality type with a blend of techniques that won't offend one personality type, while you're trying to influence the others.

Type Ones. Tim Henning is a focused Type One who will want to see the facts first without wasting any time. For this reason, you begin your presentation with a slide that shows the size of the market you're going after. You conclude with a strong statement and qualifying question: "As you can see, we have a substantial market opportunity here. How does that sound to you, Tim?" When he responds with "Great, what's next?" You know you're heading down the right track for a Type One.

Type Twos. Gary Hanson is sitting to the left of Henning and has a Type Two personality. Although, like his Type One counterpart, he likes to see the numbers, he's more guarded. He'll want to know what source you used to extract the data you're presenting before he'll give you his nod of approval. When you tell him up front during your introduction of the first slide that all of your data came from the U.S. Census Bureau, you lock in your credibility with Gary.

Type Threes. Type Threes appreciate meetings where there is a relaxed atmosphere. When Elizabeth Peers compliments you on the music, you inform her that the music is by Caballero. She politely tells you that Caballero is one of her favorite musicians. Of course, you already knew that by talking to her secretary. If your presentation has a consistent flow to it, you will impress Peers.

Type Fours. Be extra careful not to ignore your Type Four executive, Dale Mosier. Type Fours tend to not say a lot and will give you the appearance that they are on your side until you're all done with your presentation. Then, you will suddenly find out that they are not about to support you. Find out what Mosier's "hot button" is before the start of the meeting and leverage it early on in your presentation. For example, if you learned that Dale is infatuated with the Internet, present a well-designed slide that shows how you plan to create a website to support the project. When you complete this part of your presentation, stop and ask him if his staff would be interested in working with you on the development of the website. Hopefully, you will get a favorable response from him.

PERSONALITY PROFILES OF UPPER MANAGERS

By now, it should be obvious that any strategy you develop to inspire upper managers requires that you know how to recognize and interact effectively with their personality attributes. Knowledge of their personality types will help you come to terms with them. Whether you are encountering them socially or in planned settings, your ability to recognize and understand their personality types and leverage your presentation to complement their attributes will help make your encounter inspiring. Each personality type within the upper management ranks brings with it a unique set of strengths and weaknesses, which are summarized as follows:

Type One executives: Type One executives love adventure and action-oriented ideas. When you enter into a conversation with them, listen closely to what they say so that you can discover what subjects excite them. Then, structure your conversation around those subjects. Type Ones have a very narrow focus within their business. Type Ones are committed to work, goals, and high levels of productivity. They like being in power positions and demand high work standards from others. They can become very insecure if anyone with more power than they have challenges their beliefs.

Type Two executives: Creativity is important to Type Two executives. If you have ideas that you believe are creative, Type Twos will generally be receptive to them. They want their feelings to be understood and appreciated by their subordinates. Appeal to their need to be wanted by telling them you need their help and support. If they respect you, the obstacles will go away. They are subject to moods of depression and make excellent pessimists. Although they will identify reasons why a new idea won't work, they know what needs to be done to remove those reasons. Be direct and ask them the question, "What are the obstacles that I can expect to encounter on this project, and what can I do to eliminate them?" Most Type Two executives appreciate empowered employees, and if they believe you are empowered and committed to the organization, they will help you resolve the problem.

Type Three executives: Type Three executives can be hard people to inspire. They often appear to be distant or acting without direction. They're also independent thinkers and like to do their own thing. However, they like to receive any kind of recognition and support for their roles from subordinates. If you can give them what they need, you can inspire them to help you any way they can. You have to first get their attention by convincing them that your idea is worthy of their consideration through emphasizing the benefits that it would give to the organization.

Type Four executives: On the surface, Type Four executives tend to get excited about everything. Everything is a great idea to them—as long as they don't have to get involved. They like to pay "lip service" to subordinates and their ideas to avoid hurting their feelings. To get their attention and inspire them you need to find an idea that they believe is an outstanding opportunity. Type Four executives want to be popular with everyone and believe that anyone who helps them achieve their empowered objectives deserves their support. Since they do not like to work any harder than they have to, avoid getting them involved with anything that will require more work on their part.

PUTTING IT ALL TOGETHER

A leader's ability to influence, to move, or to guide by inspiration the people he encounters is an essential part of his character and an indispensable attribute of his personality. Inspiration is an exciting word. Why? Because it sparks and fuels the fire within upper management to accommodate and support the leaders they have selected to help run their organization. Upper management expects their leaders to be enthusiastic, energetic, and positive about the future. The leaders must be able to communicate their vision in ways that encourages upper management. A leader without an inspirational vision won't remain on upper managements' most wanted list for long.

Although the enthusiastic, energetic, and positive attitude of an exemplary leader may not change the context of the work that needs to be done, it certainly makes the project more meaning-ful. Whatever the circumstances, when a leader breathes life into upper management's objectives, the top level of the company will be much more willing in the future to solicit his help again. In this chapter, we showed you how to use different inspirational techniques on upper management to help move your career onto the fast track. We also covered several techniques that you can use to create encounter opportunities. Executive encounters offer you a chance to present with inspiration not only what you know, but who you are and why you are the leader they have been look-ing for.

Conclusion

I HOPE YOU have enjoyed reading *Stop Managing And Lead* and have benefited from taking the personality and needs tests to help you better understand the attributes of your personality and the personality of others. I encourage you to review this book periodically to measure how you're progressing up the leadership ladder. Read other leadership-related books that will stretch your leadership capabilities and seek out other leaders who are willing to mentor you along the way. One of the best ways to become the kind of leader for whom organizations are looking is to keep learning about leadership. It's a never-ending process. Good luck on your exciting journey into leadership.

Glossary

Achievement. A leader's need for achievement is the need to do one's best, to be successful, and to accomplish tasks that are challenging. How much effort a leader is willing to expend to achieve something he wants is directly related to his motivational level. Achievement needs can be satisfied in several different ways like winning an athletic event, working to obtain a material object like a car, or improving one's self-esteem by being promoted at work. The need for achievement is usually driven by one's own desires rather by than a collaborative effort with others.

Accountability. People who are reluctant to accept any accountability seldom move into leadership positions. When things happen to go well for them, they won't know why, but they'll grab all of the unearned credit they can get to try to establish their accountability. If things don't go their way, they will always look for someone to blame. The acceptance of accountability requires a level of competence that they don't have.

Adaptability. Leaders who are adaptable can juggle multiple demands without losing their focus on important issues. They are comfortable with the ambiguities of organizational life. They are flexible at adapting to new challenges, quick at adjusting to change, and flexible in their thinking in the face of new realities.

Affiliations. A leader draws people to her in order to solicit their cooperation in getting something done. Affiliation includes a desire to participate in group discussions or team settings rather than always working alone. Leaders with affiliation have a participative personality style and form strong bonds with their friends and associates. They like to share their feelings with others and are more comfortable making group decisions.

Attributes. Attributes are inherent characteristics that are closely associated with a leader's personality and are displayed in the way he acts. How a leader deals with the circumstances of his life tells you many things about his attributes. They are often revealed in crisis situations.

Born Leaders. Some leaders have an innate ability to enter into a new situation, size it up, instinctively say the right things, and make all the right moves. They're blessed with the ability to effectively communicate with whomever they talk to. Born leaders are experts at persuading others to do what they want them to do in any situation by creating clear and exciting visions for people to follow.

Change. Leaders understand the reasons and need for change. They can become strong advocates for a change they believe in, even in the face of opposition. Their orientation toward change depends on their personality type. Leaders know how to overcome barriers to change.

Character. The character of a leader is one of the attributes that make up her personality. A leader with a distinguished character is one who will not compromise and avoid problems. She'll stick with the right decision even though it may not be the most popular position to take.

Commitment. To a leader, the only real measure of commitment is action. When a leader commits to something, he sets up the steps he needs to take to make it happen. He creates a timeline and initiates the action. That's how he proves himself to be a committed leader. Leaders know the importance of following through on any commitments that they make.

Communication. All leaders develop excellent communication skills, which are essential to effective leadership. Without those skills, they will never become leaders. They must be able to share their messages with others in a manner that sparks their enthusiasm and motivation. If they cannot do that, having a good message won't matter. Without the ability to communicate effectively, they will never make it as a leader.

Competence. A leader's ability to plan something and do it in such a way that others have confidence in what she is doing. Because of their competence, leaders are capable of inspiring people and can rally them to support a cause.

Conflict management. Leaders who know how to manage conflicts are able to draw out the emotions of all parties involved in the conflict. They have the ability to understand the differing perspectives and then find common ground that everyone can endorse. They bring the conflict to the surface, view all sides, and then redirect the energy of those involved toward a shared solution.

Conflict style. A leader is acutely aware of the classic elements that are behind the traditional thinking and resolution of conflict: win/lose (confrontation), yield/yield (compromise), and win/win (collaboration). Great leaders exercise a win/win conflict resolution style.

Confrontations. Leaders neutralize confrontations. The word itself connotes something serious, and for this reason, leaders avoid confrontations as much as possible. They are unpleasant, disruptive to relationships, counterproductive, and can be costly to one's leadership position.

Decision Making. Leaders make decisions that are based on intuition, that essential ability to apply not just their technical expertise but their life's experiences to an issue. Decision-making comes naturally to a self-aware leader.

Delegation. A leader understands that one of the obvious benefits of delegating is that it saves time. If she can successfully delegate some of her activities to others, it frees her up to work on the things that only she can do. It also provides her with a way to give her followers challenging assignments that stretch their capabilities.

Developing Others. Leaders are adept at cultivating people's abilities and have a genuine interest in those whom they are helping. They understand the goals, personalities, strengths, and weaknesses of the people they're helping. This is why leaders are excellent mentors and coaches. By pushing people beyond their abilities, they will show more initiative and motivation to achieve goals that they thought were out of their reach.

Dominance. A leader uses dominance to control his environment, to influence or direct the behavior of others by suggesting, persuading, or commanding them to do something. When dominance is used aggressively, like forcing someone to act against his will, it can create poor morale. If it is used to reward employees, it can motivate them.

Empathy. Is an understanding leaders have. Empathetic leaders are aware of or sensitive to the feelings, thoughts, and experience of others. Because of this quality, they are able to communicate more effectively with others. They can adjust to a wide range of emotional signals, letting their senses tell them what is going on, either face to face or in a group setting. Empathy allows leaders to get along well with people of diverse backgrounds and cultures.

Empowered. Leaders who are empowered are able to encourage others to reach their highest levels of personal and professional achievement. No matter how hard a leader works, no matter how engaging her personality may be, if she is unable to work through others by means of her empowered personality, she won't make it as a leader. For over a decade, empowerment has been used as a powerful business tool. When employees feel they are contributing to an organization's success, when they can influence how things are done, and when their efforts are recognized with rewards, they are empowered. Empowerment energizes people to tackle daily challenges, to increase the quality of their work, and to improve their productivity. In the years to come, the truly successful organizations will be those that are best able to apply the creative energy of empowered individuals to achieve constant improvement.

Encountering. Leaders like to initiate encounters with others. Planned encounters offer them an opportunity to demonstrate how well versed they are in a subject that's of interest to people who could influence their career or provide them with help when it's needed. They know how to present the desired information in a format that motivates and inspires the people they encounter. Encountering their own employees gives leaders an opportunity to inspire and motivate and to keep everyone focused on the tasks at hand.

Floating Relationships. A floating relationship acts like a life raft to a leader. If he should fall overboard, his life raft is always there to save him. People with whom the leader has a floating relationship are the ones he can trust and meet with to vent his frustrations. In most floating relationships, leaders don't have to get any viable advice. Often, a few kind words are all that they may need. In the same fashion, a leader should seek to provide his employees with a floating relationship, so they know they can always come to him with problems and frustrations.

Goals. All leaders know how to establish goals that motivate people. Increasing people's expectations of reaching their goals and enhancing their personal situation is the essence of good leadership. A leader's behavior is directed toward goals, and each goal offers a benefit to the company and to the leader and his employees. Whatever goals people choose to pursue, they must believe that they are attainable.

Indispensable Leadership Attributes. Leadership is based on a set of four attributes that leaders must possess in order to be effective: The way they think and display their character, their commitment to life, and their ability to communicate from the heart with competence.

Influencing. A leader's power to influence ranges from finding just the right appeal for the person he's trying to influence to knowing how to obtain agreement to support his initiatives. Leaders who are adept in influencing people are persuasive and engaging individuals. The art of influencing occurs on two levels. At its lowest level, people will follow someone because they have to. At a higher level, people follow someone they believe in because of what he has done for them and the organization. At this level, good things happen: morale is high, needs are met, and goals are realized.

Initiative. Leaders who have a sense of what it takes to control their own destiny excel in initiative. They seize opportunities or create them rather than sit back waiting for them to happen. They are willing to cut through the red tape or bend the rules to create better possibilities for the future.

Inner-Circle Team. An inner-circle team is a leader's core team, made up of about ten people she can count on. Her top candidates can include friends, family members, and associates in her professional world who all fit within the scope of what she wants to accomplish as a leader.

Inspiration. Leaders who know how to inspire create a vision that moves people. They embody what they ask of others and are able to articulate shared visions and missions in a way that persuades people to follow them. They offer a sense of common purpose that makes work exciting.

Intimacy. Leaders foster intimacy in the relationships they develop. They prefer to develop emotional connections with others in their personal and professional lives. They'll celebrate any occasion that will help them foster intimacy with others.

Interaction. Leaders like to interact with people. Their consistent level of enthusiasm, drive, and relentless pursuit of their goals all set the tone for an organization. Their day-to-day leadership revolves around a series of interactions that require the use of different motivational techniques and strategies.

Meeting Motivators. Much of people's impatience with meetings stems from the time it takes meetings to produce real value. To avoid this problem, a leader will tell attendees what the exact purpose of the meeting is before the meeting. A real leader is very specific about what he wants to accomplish at every meeting he sponsors.

Myers-Briggs. During World War II, two renowned psychologists, Katherine Cook Briggs and Isabel Briggs Myers, her daughter, began to conduct a massive study in which people from all walks of life were interviewed to determine if the attributes of a person's personality could be categorized. The purpose of the test was originally to determine in what kinds of jobs women entering the workforce should be placed to take full advantage of their talents. Briggs and Myers concluded that people fit into one of sixteen personality types or categories. They based these categories on the work of Sigmund Freud's follower, Carl Jung. The Myers-Briggs Type Indicator (called the MBTI and published in 1962) became the most widely used assessment instrument for determining personality type. Type differences determine how we perceive and judge what's happening around us, how we get motivated, how we handle conflict, and how we use power. Astute leaders learn how to take all of these factors into consideration so that they are in a better position to lead and influence the people in their organization to achieve success.

Motivation. A leader has reasons for everything she does. She does not act blindly and will set up goals in her never-ending attempt to get what she wants and to keep herself motivated. A motivated leader motivates everyone she touches to help improve the overall performance of the organization. When she practices this style of leadership, her employees are much more productive, it is easier to get them to help each other, and they themselves stay motivated.

Needs. All leaders, as well as employees, have needs that demand satisfaction and that are expressed in their personalities. There are three need categories that play an important role in how leaders manage tasks and develop their relations with each other:
Achievement—the act of accomplishment brought about by one's effort.
Dominance—the act of exerting influence over other people.
Affiliation—the act of developing a close connection or relationship with someone.

Network. To a leader, a network is an organized collection of personal contacts that he relies on when he needs help or information. He may meet a person at a meeting or social function who may not have a direct fit into his leadership plan. However, if his intuition tells him this person is worth knowing, he will include her in his network.

Observation. A good leader observes more than what people say. She observes changes in their voice inflections, speaking manner, eye contact, facial expressions, posture, and body movement. Observing the way people act is one of the best ways to determine their personality type.

Opportunities. Opportunities are everywhere, and successful leaders know where to look for them. They use them to get a real jump on their leadership goals by becoming problem solvers, which are where the real opportunities can be found in any organization. For every problem an organization has, there is an opportunity for a leader who can come up with a solution. Recognition is awarded to the provider of solutions.

Optimism. A leader who is optimistic can roll with the punches and sees opportunities rather than setbacks around every corner. He sees others in a positive rather than negative light and expects the best of them. His outlook leads him to expect that changes in the future will make things better. To an optimist, everything happens for the best.

Organizational Awareness. A leader with keen organizational awareness is politically astute, able to detect crucial and often hidden networks and recognize key power relationships. She understands the political forces that are at work within an organization, as well as the guiding values, and unspoken rules that operate among the people in the organization.

Personal Hooks. The personal hook is one of the most effective communication tools leaders use. Whenever possible, a leader will incorporate something that is personally important to the person he is communicating with to hold her attention.

Personality Types. Understanding what makes up the sixteen personality types is more than most people are willing to digest. The Myers-Briggs team recognized this problem, and in subsequent studies they consolidated their findings into four primary personality types. These are the types that astute leaders recognize.

Persuasion. Persuasion is the art of guiding someone through a logical progression of thoughts so that he can arrive at a conclusion that complements a leader's view. In essence, a leader's use of persuasion enables the other person to understand what they are saying and become motivated to do what is in their best interest to do. The art of persuading others is, in many respects, a communication game. The more ideas leaders are able to sell with their persuasive words, the more people will think of them as contributors to the organization.

Power Attribute. A leader knows how to control the power attributes of her personality so that it does not interfere with her goals and objectives.

Type Ones and Twos have power-based personalities and expend a lot of energy preserving the balance of power in their relationships. Type Threes and Fours will often play the role of "bench warmers" who like to sit on the sidelines watching the power players vie for position.

Power Relationships. Power relationships, if they are properly used, can provide leaders with the people they need to help them accelerate up the leadership ladder. When two people get together in a power relationship setting, they instantly surround themselves with a sphere of energy that allows them to tap into each other for ideas.

Presentations. They can be formal or informal. If a leader is about to make a formal presentation in front of a group, she knows it is absolutely critical that the first one minute of her presentation be viewed as positive rather than negative. First impressions begin with what others see in the presenter. The more you know about the culture and personality types of your audience, the more accurately you can predict their expectations and tailor the presentation to create a favorable impression. The same principles apply to informal presentations.

Proactive Leaders. Good proactive leaders constantly monitor the dynamic changes occurring in their business environments, from consumer buying patterns to strategic maneuvers of competitors. They listen carefully to what upper management is telling them and respond accordingly with the motivational drive that gets the job done.

Questions. Leaders know how to ask people the right questions and listen carefully to what they have to say, observing their nonverbal behavior. Answers to questions afford astute leaders the chance to gain insights into a person's personality type. The question is a powerful communication tool. Leaders know how to get someone's attention by using question hooks, which are very specific questions designed to get the listener to think carefully before he responds. Question hooks works well on individuals who have short attention spans. The purpose of the question hook is to take the listener's mind off whatever he was doing before hearing the question. Answers to question hooks provide leaders with information they can use to persuade their target to do something.

Relationships. Success in leadership is a function of how well leaders work with and relate to all of the people who are in their domain. Skilled leaders have resonance with a wide circle of people and have a knack for building rapport with them. They know how to sustain solid relationships that enable them to get extraordinary things done on a regular basis. They work under the realization that nothing important gets done alone. Therefore, they have networks in place that they can call on when they need support.

Selling. A good leader is always selling his ideas and beliefs. He understands that life itself is a selling game every day of the year, twenty-four hours a day. He's constantly testing his selling skills by asking, "Did I sell any of my ideas today?" Leaders know they can't promote themselves if they don't sell their ideas every day.

Self-Assessment. Leaders who assess themselves exhibit a gracefulness in learning, understanding where they need to improve and welcoming constructive criticism. They know when to ask for help and what they need to do to cultivate new leadership strengths.

Self-Assurance. Type One leaders are the most outwardly self-assured of all the personality types, but they also tend to be highly insecure individuals. They would be better off if they lowered the high expectations they have set for themselves and worked on reducing their inherent insecurities. Type Twos and Threes need to control their tendency to self-criticism, which depresses their self-assurance. They should concentrate more on developing positive characteristics. Type Fours can get so wrapped up in their own self-satisfaction that it becomes difficult for them to know when they make mistakes. They need to be aware of this situation and work at developing healthy self-assurance.

Self-Awareness. Leaders high in self-awareness are attuned to their inner signals and recognize how their feelings affect their job performance. They are attuned to their guiding values and can see the big picture in complex situations. Self-aware leaders are candid and are able to speak openly about their emotions and with conviction about their vision. They exhibit a gracefulness in learning where they need to improve and welcome constructive criticism and feedback.

Self-Confidence. If a hole opens up in a leader's confidence that she is not aware of or ignores, she may walk ploddingly down the path and lose the motivation she once had. Successful leaders refuse to let this happen because they know that if they lose their self-confidence, their leadership progress will stop. They'll move quickly to fill any holes in their confidence level as soon as they're discovered so that they can continue moving up the leadership ladder.

Self-Control. Leaders who practice self-control find ways to manage their emotions and impulses. They are capable of staying calm and stable during a crisis or a trying situation. They'll openly admit mistakes and confront unethical behavior in others rather than turn a blind eye.

Self-Esteem. Self-esteem means feeling good about yourself and is a critical component of a leader's character. All personality types seek self-esteem in everything they do. Feeling good is at best a difficult human characteristic to measure. Psychologists generally believe that Types Ones and Fours have higher inherent self-esteem levels than Type Twos and Threes. The reason is because Type Twos and Threes are more prone to self-criticism. Type Ones and Fours are often so busy criticizing others that they seldom have any time to do any self-analysis, let alone self-criticism.

Self-Motivation. What does it take to have the self-motivation of an effective leader? The key is the ability to focus on goal-oriented priorities. The ongoing successful completion of goals generates the fuel that drives an individual's motivation. Without the attainment of goals, there is no motivation. Unfortunately, the most common self-motivational problem leaders have is their lack of concentration. They know what they need to do but somehow, it never gets done. For some reason, they are not motivated.

Service. Leaders who value service monitor customer and client satisfaction to ensure they are getting the level of service that they deserve and need.

Sinking Relationships. A sinking relationship is like dead weight that is either dragging a leader down, holding her back, or sinking her altogether. It's a relationship with a person who has low self-esteem and is often avoided by others like the plague. Such people can become argumentative with anyone who disagrees with them and as a result, refuse to listen to other people's ideas. They tend to dwell on events that have already happened and will use them to make unrealistic projections about what they believe will happen in the future. No leader has the time to nurture sinking relationships.

Social Encounters. The pen is mightier than the sword, but neither is mightier than the mouth, especially when it comes to creating first impressions with people in social encounters. Vocal communication is second only to body language as a means of communicating in social settings. In face-to-face interactions, it isn't enough for leaders to be physically attractive. The moment they speak, they either confirm or deny the initial impression they've created. If they sound harsh and abrasive, they probably will be viewed as harsh and abrasive. If they sound timid and insecure, they will be considered as such. And, if they sound strong and confident, chances are they'll be thought of that way.

Teamwork. Leaders know how to form teams to generate an atmosphere of friendly cooperation, self-respect, and a desire to achieve the objectives of the team. They know how to draw others outside of the team to actively and enthusiastically support the team's effort. They spend time developing close relationships with team members that go beyond mere working obligations.

Time Management. The effective use of a leader's time is critical to his success. How he uses his time will determine what impact he'll have on his organization. He uses several techniques to improve his use of time. For example, he will often arrive at work early in the morning before anyone else so he can work without interruption. He likes to prepare detailed schedules to maximize his use of time.

Transparency. This is the openness that a leader shows to others about her feelings, beliefs, and actions. She possesses integrity and will openly admit mistakes in her never-ending drive for self-improvement.

Type Indicator Test. The test was based on the Myers-Briggs Type Indicators (MBTI) that world-renowned psychologists Dr. Myers and Dr. Briggs developed in the period from World War II to the 1960s. MBTI's enormous appeal stemmed in part from its simplicity. The questions on the test did, in fact, assess one's personality with a surprising degree of accuracy. But like a miracle diet, it lured some leaders into expecting it to be a quick fix. A person's personality type is only one piece of the puzzle. To complete the puzzle, leaders must understand how an individual's personality affects his inspirational and motivational drive to establish goals and his relationships with others. Leaders know what the dominant as well as the less-dominant attributes are in their own personalities as well as the personalities of those they rely on. Armed with this knowledge, they are in a much better position to come to terms not only with themselves but with people whose personality types and styles are different from theirs.

Index

Accountability, coaching, 171–74
Achievement, need for, 37–38, 39–40
Advice, persuading for, 199–200
Affiliation, need for, 37–39, 41
Arrogant bosses, influencing, 218–21
Benefits, persuading with, 189–91
Bosses. *See* Influencing bosses;
    Inspiring (upper management)
Bureaucrats, influencing, 212–15
Chameleons, influencing, 223–25
Change, coaching, 174–78
Change, confronting, 150–53
Character motivators, 123–24
Coaching, 161–81
    accountability, 171–74
    attributes by personality type,
        160, 163–66, 167–71, 172–74,
        176–78, 179–80
    benefits of, 161, 181
    change, 174–78
    employees to learn, 166–71
    how leaders coach, 161–62
    new leaders, 162–66
    team rejects, 178–80
Commitment, 2, 4–9
    assessing, 25
    empowering, 74–76
    improving abilities of, 6–9
    motivators, 124–26
    personality trait qualities of, 70
    qualities of, 5–6
Communication, 2, 9–14
    empowering, 76–79
    hooks, 77–79, 109
    importance of, 9–10
    improving skills, 11–14
    personality trait qualities of, 70

persuading with, 186–89
presidents exemplifying, 9
qualities of, 10–11
Competence, 2, 14–17, 70
Competence motivators, 129–30
Confidence, 20, 21–22
Confrontations, 23–24, 139–59
    attributes by personality type,
        138, 144–45, 146–50, 151–53,
        154–55, 156–58
    how they start, 140–41
    importance of controlling,
        139–40, 158–59
    who confronters are, 141–43
Confronting
    change, 150–53
    dishonesty, 145–48
    financial problems, 153–55
    layoffs, 155–58
    nearly retired people, 143–45
    prima donnas, 148–50
Cooperation, persuading for,
    201–3
Decision making, 22
Dishonesty, confronting, 145–48
Dominance, need for, 37–39, 40
Drive, discipline, direction, 80–82
Emotional fortitude, 24
Empowerment, 71–82
    art of, 72–73
    of commitment, 74–76
    of communication, 76–79
    of competence, 80–82
Encounters
    fast-track, 244–46
    inspiring, 235–36
    social, 242–44

strategic, 236–39
sudden, 239–42
Ethos/pathos/logos, 205–6
Financial problems, confronting, 153–55
Firefighters, influencing, 227–29
Glossary, 251–61
Goals, 85–99
    attributes by personality type, 84, 88–90, 91–94, 95–99
    defining, 89–90, 99
    importance of, 85–86
    mixing, 90–92
    owning, 93–94
    personality types and, 84, 88–90, 91–94, 96–99
    setting, 23, 87–89
    setting, for employees, 94–99
    working on, 92–93
Impressions, inspiring, 232–35
Influencing bosses, 205–29
    arrogant managers, 218–21
    attributes by personality type, 204, 208–12, 213–15, 216–17, 219–21, 222–23, 224–25, 226–27, 228–29
    basics of, 206–7
    bureaucrats, 212–15
    chameleons, 223–25
    ethos/pathos/logos and, 205–6
    firefighters, 227–29
    lone rangers, 225–27
    macromanagers, 210–12
    micromanagers, 207–10
    power addicts, 221–23
    unscrupulous managers, 215–17
Inspiring (upper management), 231–49
    attributes by personality type, 230, 237–39, 240–44, 245–46
    benefits/importance of, 231–32, 248–49
    encounters. See Encounters
    impressions, 232–35
    upper manager personality profiles and, 246–48

Layoffs, confronting, 155–58
Leadership
    assessing skills. See Self-assessment/-understanding
    desire for, 25–26
    development process, 26–27
    historical perspective, 3–4
    indispensable qualities of, 4–18. See also Commitment; Communication; Competence
    potential, 1, 4, 27–28, 250
    Sam Walton illustrating, 19–20
Lone rangers, influencing, 225–27
Macromanagers, influencing, 210–12
Meeting motivators, 132–34
Micromanagers, influencing, 207–10
Mixed personalities, 67–69
Motivating
    Type Ones, 48–50, 118, 124, 125, 127–28, 129, 132, 134, 135–36
    Type Twos, 55–56, 118, 124, 125–26, 128, 129–30, 132, 134, 136
    Type Threes, 61–62, 118, 124, 126, 128, 130, 132, 134, 136
    Type Fours, 66–67, 118, 124, 126, 128, 130, 132, 134, 136
Motivation, 119–37
    assessment quiz, 120–21
    attributes by personality type, 118, 124, 125–26, 127–28, 129–30, 131–32, 134, 135–36
    character motivators, 123–24
    commitment motivators, 124–26
    communication, 126–28
    competence, 129–30
    leadership attributes and, 122–23
    meeting motivators, 132–34
    people motivators, 135–36
    power of, 119–20, 136–37
    team motivators, 130–32
Need(s)
    achievement as, 37–38, 39–40
    affiliation as, 37–39, 41
    assessment test, 37–39
    dominance as, 37–39, 40
    essential, 36–37

Opportunities, recognizing, 22
People motivators, 135–36
Personality
    determining your style, 41–42
    essential needs and, 36–37
    leadership, summarized, 24–25
    test, taking and interpreting,
        30–33
Personality types, 43–69. *See also
    specific Type references*
    importance of understanding,
        30–31, 69
    mixed, 67–69
    needs/wants, strengths/weaknesses
        chart, 68
    quality traits of, 70
    of upper managers, 246–48
Persuading peers, 185–203
    for advice, 199–200
    attributes by personality type,
        184, 187–89, 190–91, 193–94,
        196–98, 199–200, 202–3
    with benefits, 189–91
    with communication, 186–89
    for cooperation, 201–3
    importance of, 186
    with justification, 192–94
    for support, 194–98
Pessimists, avoiding, 112–15
"Positiveness," 113–15
Power addicts, influencing, 221–23
Pressure, handling, 23
Prima donnas, confronting, 148–50
Relationships, 101–17
    attributes by personality type,
        100, 103–5, 106–8
    avoiding pessimists, 112–15
    cultural connectedness and,
        115–16
    establishing network of, 108–12
    floating, 104–5
    importance of, 101–2, 117, 137
    mixed types of, 106–7
    personality types and, 100, 103–5,
        106–8

power, 105–6
    sinking, 103–4
    types of, 102–7
Self-assessment/-understanding
    importance of, 29–30
    inner journey for, 20
    motivation assessment, 120–21
    needs assessment, 37–39
    questions to ask, qualities to
        cultivate, 21–26
Team motivators, 130–32
Team rejects, coaching, 178–80
Time management, 110–12
Type Ones (power players), 43–50
    brief description, 34–35
    executives, 247
    profile of, 44–45
    quality traits of, 70
    strengths/weaknesses, 45–48
Type Twos (team players), 50–56
    brief description, 35
    executives, 247
    profile of, 50–52
    quality traits of, 70
    strengths/weaknesses, 52–55
Type Threes (diplomatic players),
    56–62
    brief description, 35–36
    executives, 247–48
    profile of, 57–58
    quality traits of, 70
    strengths/weaknesses, 58–61
Type Fours (party players), 62–67
    brief description, 36
    executives, 248
    profile of, 63
    quality traits of, 70
    strengths/weaknesses, 63–66
Unscrupulous bosses, influencing,
    215–17
Upper management. *See* Encounters;
    Inspiring (upper management)